# Administering the Successful Vocational Education Program

# Administering the Successful Vocational Education Program

William H. Bentley

Parker Publishing Company, Inc.
West Nyack, N.Y.

**Library of Congress Cataloging in Publication Data**

Bentley, William H
   Administering the successful vocational
education program.

   Includes index.
   1.  Vocational education--Administration.
I.  Title.
LC1047.8.B46      379'.155     76-30411
ISBN 0-13-005173-X

Printed in the United States of America

This book is dedicated to my wife Marie, without whose encouragement, patience, and understanding it could not have been written; to Miss Mary Daunoy, who helped with proofing and correcting the manuscript; and to the many vocational teachers and administrators with whom I have been associated for many years and from whom I have learned so much.

# The Practical Value of This Book

This book provides a broad range of tried and successful techniques for use in vocational educational administration. As a helpful ready reference for educators, it will be valuable for all administrators who search for new techniques and better ways to apply more traditional methods.

These practical approaches have been selected from the most effective programs developed during three decades of actual experience. Most have been tested by the author, some by other experienced educators. Varying conditions may require modification in some procedures, but they can easily be adapted to meet your needs.

Sequence of the material is arranged, as much as is feasible, in the order needed to operate a successful vocational program. First, a systematic procedure for determining vocational education needs will be described. You are then shown how to select and organize an advisory or steering team and given step-by-step procedures for planning and conducting a needs survey. Samples of survey instruments are shown, with instructions for developing your own if necessary. How to compile survey data, evaluate, interpret and prepare the report is described and explained in detail. You are shown how to identify needs, determine objectives, make a job analysis to determine the skills needed in a particular occupation, and how to prepare a course outline. Unless you are knowledgeable regarding a particular occupation being planned, it is necessary to secure assistance from someone who is. How to find and recruit such help is discussed in detail.

Funding vocational education is sometimes a complex problem, and often school administrators are unable to obtain such funds as are available, simply because they have difficulty in preparing a successful proposal and application. A sample proposal, which was funded, is shown with a step-by-step description of its preparation.

A key factor in any education is, of course, the ability of the teacher. Since many vocational teachers must be recruited directly from industry in order to find those with adequate occupational experience, it is often difficult to locate, screen and recruit such teachers. This book tells you what to do to find qualified teachers and how to develop an effective orientation and inservice training program for those who have not had professional educational preparation.

Implementing a vocational course requires more than most academic courses. The administrator must see that facilities are built or remodeled to meet the needs of each course. Equipment specifications must be prepared, bids taken, equipment purchased and installed in accordance with industrial standards and safety requirements. Detailed examples of various types of facilities are shown and sample specifications for both equipment and supplies will help you avoid many of the pitfalls frequently encountered. Recruitment and selection of students is an important factor in implementing a course, so various selection techniques are discussed and explained, including the use of aptitude and interest measuring instruments.

Curriculum development for vocational courses assumes major importance when you consider that for many courses no textbook is available. Especially in the craft courses, when the teacher comes directly from industry without adequate educational preparation, the administrator must be able to help him in developing a curriculum. Step by step you are shown how to identify the concepts to be taught and organize them into proper sequence for effective training. Formats of vocational guides are illustrated and orientation of teachers in their use is explained. Though this book is primarily addressed to the administrator of a comprehensive public high school, it will also be found helpful for administrators of vocational education programs in junior high school and special vocational schools.

Finally, since evaluation of program effectiveness is essential to program improvement, various evaluation techniques are discussed, with emphasis on product performance measurement through use of follow-up practices. Sample forms are shown.

*William H. Bentley*

# Table of Contents

15

**EFFECTIVELY PROMOTING AND UPDATING VOCATIONAL EDUCATION (con't)**

**11. TECHNIQUES AND STRATEGIES FOR CONTINUING GROWTH**

# Administering the Successful
# Vocational Education Program

# 1

# How to Determine Your Vocational Education Needs

**CHAPTER 1** The first step in developing a strong vocational program is to find out what is needed to give the young people of your school and community the help they need to prepare for gainful employment. Some questions come immediately to mind. What kind of gainful employment is available in the community? In the surrounding area? In the state? Are the persons whom you are to train interested in the kinds of jobs that are available? Will the employers work with you or against you in developing the program? The only way to find out is to investigate. It would be extremely rash for the administrator to undertake this task singlehanded. Let's bring some other people from the community into the picture and get them involved.

## HOW TO ORGANIZE
## AN EFFECTIVE ADVISORY COMMITTEE

Let's first take a look at what an advisory committee is and what it does? Administrative authority for vocational education is vested in the State Boards of Education and in local Boards of Education. Advisory committees are organized to advise and

27

counsel the school administrators, and to make suggestions and recommendations for their guidance in perfecting occupational education. It is their function to provide closer cooperation and better understanding of vocational education in industry, the home, and the school by providing a two-way system of communication between the school and the community—which is essential to all educational programs. No educational advisory committee has any administrative authority or responsibility. Its only function is to give advice.

A general advisory committee provides the school administrators with the following services:

1. Helps determine the need for training.
2. Recommends implementation and/or expansion of vocational programs to meet the needs.
3. Advises the Board of Education in establishing objectives and determining policies for vocational education.
4. Helps gain community support.
5. Advises the board concerning the relative emphasis on the various types of programs.
6. Promotes a desirable relationship with the public.

A program advisory committee is desirable for each occupational program. These committees are composed of members who are active in the occupation for which training is provided. They provide additional and more specific advisory counsel to the local administrator, such as:

1. Qualifications of teachers. (Most states set only the minimum standards which local districts may increase.)
2. Facility layout and selection of equipment.
3. Selection of instructional materials.
4. Standards of proficiency to be met by students in order to qualify for completion certificates.
5. Standards for selection of students.

6. Assistance in determining skills and related technology to be taught.
7. Recruitment of teachers.
8. Assistance to teacher in keeping up to date.
9. Judgment of student performance in club con
10. Placement of students after training.

Whose responsibility is it to establish an advisory c mittee? In the smaller school systems it may be the super tendent or his assistant. Most larger districts have an a ministrator or director of vocational education to whom this responsibility is usually delegated. Securing competent advisory members is an important and sometimes difficult problem. One of the best ways of recruiting an effective committee is to select persons who are interested in the success of the program and who have the abilities needed to help accomplish this success.

Which people in your community are more likely to be interested and able to assist in the preparation of young people for employment than their future employers? So the main source of committee members are the business men and women of the community. Some of the characteristics you will look for are these:

1. Intelligence, social vision, and leadership experience.
2. Interest and willingness to work for success of the program.
3. Good character and integrity.
4. Knowledge of the occupations for which education is planned.
5. Time to devote to helping the school.

Where can you find persons with these qualifications? The local Chamber of Commerce is largely composed of these people. Most local service clubs are meeting places for them. If you are not a member of at least one service club in your community, you should be—and I advise you to join. The associations formed through these clubs can greatly enhance your effectiveness in promoting vocational education to the community. Talk to these people. Explain your planned program and ask if they are willing to help you make it effective. Most of them are eager to serve if properly approached. When you have found those whom you desire to have on the committee, present their names and qualifications to the superintendent for recommendation to the Board of Education for approval. A letter of appointment and expression of appreciation for service should be sent to each member by the chairman of the board or by the superintendent.

The number of members will vary, depending largely on the size of the local district. For a small or medium size school system it is usually best to have no fewer than five nor more than nine members. In the larger systems there may be as many as thirty, most often with an executive board and sub-committees.

Proper organization of an advisory committee is essential for maximum beneficial utilization. There are many patterns of organization from which to choose and they are always varied from school to school, due to local conditions. The procedures described in this book have worked well for the author but may not be the ones that you will find most effective. Therefore, these should be understood for what they are—guides only.

After the committee members have been selected, a time for the first organizational meeting must be set, a meeting place reserved, and an agenda prepared. The meeting time should be determined with the convenience of the majority of the members in mind. Generally the evening is most suitable; a good many meet at noon for luncheon; and a few find breakfast meetings more convenient. If adequate meeting space is available at the school, and the school is centrally located and therefore convenient for the members, it is usually preferred. The meeting place should be furnished with a conference table large enough to accommodate all the members, comfortable chairs, and preferably there should be a blackboard available. Ash trays, water pitchers, and glasses should be on the table with scratch pads and pencils at each place. Coffee is often provided, depending on the custom of the community. The first agenda is almost always prepared by the school administrator, since there is no chairman or president as yet. A sample agenda for an organizational meeting is shown here, as well as organization charts suitable for a large district or a small district. Notification of the meeting, with a copy of the agenda, should be sent to each member at least a week before the meeting.

## DEVELOPING SURVEY INSTRUMENTS FOR LOCAL USE

One of the most effective means of determining local community needs for occupational education is to make a survey. Before you begin the survey it is wise to find out if a recent one has been made. It may be that the local employment office already has one on file that will answer most of your questions. If so, to duplicate their effort is a waste of time. There is no need to re-invent the wheel or to re-discover fire. Most frequently, however, you will find that while some information is available, there is still other information you need. Seldom is it possible to find an instrument that exactly meets your needs— that gives just the information you want. In this case, you must develop your own questionnaire.

How do you go about developing a questionnaire? First, determine exactly what you need to know and what questions will best elicit the facts you want. The questionnaire need not be long or complex. In fact, the briefer and simpler you make it, the more likely you are to receive a large return of answers. It is very important that you take great care to word the questions exactly to make sure they cannot be misunderstood. A multiple choice answer is desirable, if possible—for two reasons: it makes it much easier for the respondent to answer quickly and easily, and it is much easier to tabulate the answers for an analysis of the survey.

There are two types of occupational need surveys commonly used. One is the general survey to determine what kinds of occupational opportunities are available in the community. The other is used when it is necessary to determine if a specific oc-

INITIAL MEETING OF THE GENERAL ADVISORY
COMMITTEE FOR VOCATIONAL EDUCATION
Place: Board Room, Smithville Public Schools
Administration Building
Time: 7:30 p.m., March 15, 19___
Temporary Chairman: John Jones, Vocational Director
*******
AGENDA

1. Call to order.
2. Welcome and expression of appreciation by superintendent.
3. Introduction and background information of members.
4. Explanation of the function of the committee and how it can assist the school.
5. A brief history and background of the school and of the vocational education program.
6. School philosophy and objectives.
7. Philosophy and objectives of vocational education.
8. Brief overview of the present vocational education program.
9. Brief outline of the planned vocational program and the problems to be solved.
10. Committee organization:
    Select chairman and secretary.
    Set time and dates of meetings.
    Appoint committee to develop constitution and by-laws for committee.
11. Adjourn.

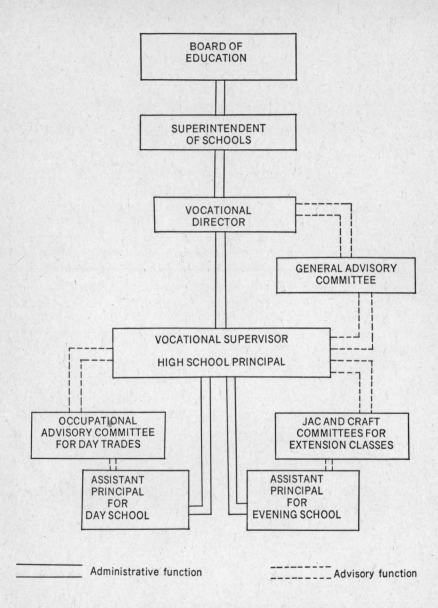

**Chart 1. Organizational Chart for Advisory Committees in Large School Systems**

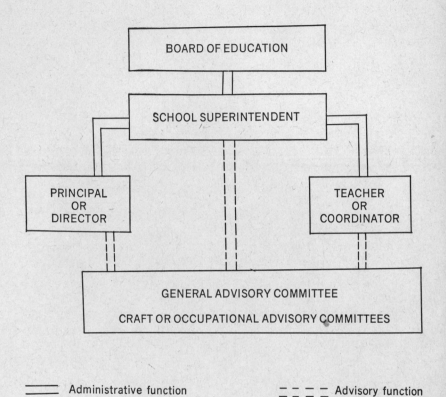

**Chart 2. Organizational Chart for Advisory Committees in Small School Systems**

cupational education is needed. The first is most often used when starting a new program where none has existed previously, while the latter is used when additional courses are considered for an existing program.

Let's look at a hypothetical case. Smithville school administrators believe that vocational education is needed in the public secondary schools of this community. Statistics are available from a recent survey and inventory made by the State Employment Commission which supports this belief and provides most of the information needed to make a decision. Only two main questions remain to be answered. How will the employers in the community accept and support the program, and what type of occupational training is most needed at this time? Shown on the following two pages is a simple questionnaire which will give answers to these questions.

## WHAT TO DO IN PLANNING
## AND CONDUCTING A SURVEY

After the survey instrument has been prepared, the next step is conducting the survey. Who should be sent the questionnaires? The persons whose input will be most valuable are those who employ workers in the occupations being considered. Do not limit yourself to only those in the community served by your school district but include adjacent communities if there is potential employment opportunity there for your students. Distribution is usually by mail in all except the smallest communities. It is best to enclose a brief letter of explanation with each instrument, and be sure to include a stamped, self-addressed envelope for the reply. Attention to the proper approach will help assure a larger percentage of returned answers. If you anticipate less than a 75% response on a large number of questionnaires some saving can be effected by using Business Reply envelopes for the response, since you pay postage for only those actually returned, though at a higher rate. If only a small number is sent the saving is insignificant. In very small communities it is often more desirable to personally interview those

GENERAL SURVEY OF COMMUNITY VOCATIONAL NEEDS*

The Administrators of ~~Smithville~~ Public Schools are considering the expansion of a vocational education program and are trying to determine the specific occupational training needs of this community. You can help us make this decision by completing and returning this short questionnaire. We appreciate your assistance.

1. Do you believe that this community needs occupational training as a part of the public education program? (Please underline your answer.)

   Yes     Perhaps     Undecided     No

2. What kind of occupational education do you believe is needed? (Check those listed and/or list others.)

   | | | |
   |---|---|---|
   | Auto Mechanic | Auto Body & Paint | Cosmetology |
   | Drafting | Electrician | Electronic Technician |
   | Plumbing | Refrigeration | Air Conditioning |
   | Pipefitting | Carpentry | Bricklaying |
   | Printing | Photography | Office & Clerical |
   | Food Service | Health Occupations | Sales & Distribution |

   List other occupations here and make comments or suggestions._____

   _____
   _____

3. How many persons do you employ and in what kind of jobs?

   _____
   _____

4. If trained young people were available, would you give them preference in employment?

   Yes     Probably     Undecided     Doubtful     No

   Approximately how many employees do you hire each year?

   1 - 5     5 - 10     10 - 20     20 - 50     Over 50

   ---

   * To be sent to all major employers in the community.

## SURVEY TO DETERMINE NEED TO TRAIN MACHINISTS

Smithville Public Schools are considering implementing an educational program to train machinist and related workers if it is determined that such a program is needed in this community. You can help us make this decision by answering the following questions. Thank you for your time and assistance.

1. How many employees do you have in each of these jobs?

   Machinist_____Machine Operator_____
   Toolmaker_____Helper_____

2. How many employees do you expect to hire in these jobs each year?

   1 - 5____; 5 - 10____; 10 - 20____; 20 - 50____;
   Over 50_____

3. Do you believe that a machinist training program would be helpful to you? (Underline your answer.)

   Yes     Probably     Don't Know     Doubtful     No

4. Would you employ those who had completed training?

   Yes     Probably     Don't Know     Doubtful     No

5. Do you have suggestions or recommendations? Comment below.

_____

_____

_____

_____

_____

_____

_____

being surveyed. When only a very small number of responses is possible, much more accurate and complete information can be obtained by personal contact. In any case, always express appreciation for the time and assistance given, even if the response is negative.

## HOW TO COMPILE AND INTERPRET
## SURVEY RESULTS

When the questionnaires have been completed and returned, you are ready to compile the results into information that you can use. One of the simplest ways to do this is to take a blank survey form and beside each choice indicate the number of positive responses to that item. This is simple with multiple choice or other types of check-list answers. When the question requires an unstructured answer, each response must be interpreted and classified and this takes more time. Write down each answer in its simplest form, and each time it occurs use a tally mark. Care must be taken to include in each classification all the answers that have the same meaning though worded differently. Comments should be listed in order of frequency.

After responses have been classified and tabulated, you are ready to interpret the data. The important factors to be considered are these: Is there enough need for this program to justify it? Will jobs be available for those who complete the training satisfactorily? Will this job market continue in the foreseeable future? To what skill level must workers be trained to fill the kind of jobs available? Are there programs presently in progress that can fill this need? This last question requires an additional step. A review of the programs you now have must be made.

Interpretation of "enough need" to justify operating a program depends on many factors. The principal factors are how many students are to be trained each year and the number of jobs that will be available. In making this decision it will be necessary to take into account all other sources of worker supply, and probable rate of growth. Related employment must also be considered. A general rule of thumb followed by some administrators is that if the probable job openings each year in both the occupation and related employment closely approximate or exceed the anticipated total of workers available from all sources, the program is justified. If there is an excess of workers from present sources for anticipated employment opportunities, it is usually inadvisable to develop the training program.

## REVIEWING CURRENT VOCATIONAL PROGRAMS AND MAKING RECOMMENDATIONS

In reviewing your present program a follow-up study is almost mandatory. It is the best method of evaluating the effectiveness of skill training. By follow-up, I mean finding out how many of those who have completed the program are employed in the occupation for which they were trained or in related jobs. Equally important is how they have progressed in their chosen career. Can this progress be attributed to the training received at school? This follow-up should be an ongoing and continuous process for at least five years after a student leaves the program. Many experienced educators do conduct follow-up to some extent, though in most cases inadequately. In Chapter Nine we will discuss and explain the techniques of organizing and conducting an effective follow-up system.

In reviewing the present program, ask yourself if you already have a program that with some modification or redirection could adequately meet the need that you have discovered. For example, if you find that you have a general metal trades course teaching a cluster of related metal-working skills, including machine operation, sheet metal fabrication, and welding, the follow-up study may show that very few are employed as sheet metal workers, that most of those who majored in welding are placed, but that there are never enough machine operation majors to fill the demand. In such a case it may be desirable to reduce the emphasis on sheet metal and concentrate more heavily on machine work. It may be that the need for machine shop workers can be met in the present program by providing more intense training in machine operation skills.

After the needs assessment is completed and evaluated and the present program has been reviewed, the decision can be made as to what will best solve the needs. This course of action is presented as a proposal to the superintendent for his approval and for submission to the Board of Education for their approval. If there is more than one practical solution, and there frequently is, it is often wise to submit several alternative courses of action, recommended in order of their desirability. When the superintendent and the Board of Education have considered the recommendations and have given approval, you are ready to plan the program in detail.

> *Author's note:* The procedures and techniques of organizing advisory committees described above are those used by the author and are based largely on adaptation and modification of those found in the uncopyrighted pamphlet published by the U.S. Office of Education. This booklet, which will be extremely helpful to those who need a more indepth treatment of this subject, may be obtained by writing to the following address: Sam W. King, *Organization and Effective Use of Advisory Committees* (Washington D.C., U.S. Office of Education), Vocational Division No. 288, OE-84009.

# 2

# What to Do
# When Planning
# Vocational Education

**CHAPTER 2** In planning a vocational course to be offered, it is first necessary to identify the specific skills to be developed and the technical knowledge to be learned. Until this step is complete, you cannot determine the equipment and tools needed, the reference library required, or even the size of the physical facility.

## HOW TO IDENTIFY SPECIFIC TRAINING NEEDS AND DETERMINE OBJECTIVES

If you are starting a course that is offered in many schools in your state, it is probable that a course outline is already available from the state education agency, along with a suggested equipment list, needed references, etc. It is always worthwhile to check with the state agency for any material that may be available in planning. Certainly if such material is already available, even if some modification and adjustment are needed to meet your special needs, you can save a lot of otherwise wasted time and effort. However, if you find that such material is not available, you must develop this information for yourself. If

43

the occupational education you are planning is offered in only a few schools or if it is a new area of training, it is very likely that no standard course of study exists. In this case you are starting from scratch. This can be tedious and time consuming unless a carefully planned procedure is followed. This procedure, variously called occupational analysis, trade analysis, or job analysis, is necessary before a course of study can be prepared. Let's see how this is done.

### STEP-BY-STEP PROCEDURE
### FOR JOB ANALYSIS

Job analysis means breaking down the job or job family for which training is to be offered into its smallest components, usually identified as operations. Each operation can be divided into "do skills" and "know skills." The "do skill" is the psychomotor behavior required to perform the operation and the "know skill" is the cognitive knowledge necessary. Though affective learning is an important part of occupational education, it is not usually included in a job analysis for planning purposes since it requires no special equipment or facility.

Unless you are personally very knowledgeable in this particular occupation, it is essential that you have the assistance of someone who is. In fact, even if you are or have been employed in this job, it is very helpful to have one or preferably two other people work with you on an analysis to make sure that no operation is omitted. Your craft advisory committee is a good source for subject matter specialists. If the person who will teach the course is known, ask him to help. If volunteer assistance is not readily available, a skilled person in the occupation can be employed as a consultant, and is well worth the expense, since by proper planning you can not only develop a better program but also save the cost of purchasing unnecessary equipment that contributes little to skill development.

### Step One

Always start with a comprehensive job description. One of the best sources for this is the *Dictionary of Occupational Titles,* published by the federal government. If you do not have a copy, it is available from almost every public library. From such a job description you can develop what is called by professional programmers of instruction a "terminal behavior repertoire," which is only the sixty-four dollar way to say what performance skills the student is expected to have after training. Let's look at a typical job description in the D.O.T. and see how it can be used.

> PLUMBER (const.) 862.381. Assembles, installs, and repairs pipes, fittings, and fixtures of heating, water, and drainage systems, according to specifications and plumbing codes: studies building plans and working drawings to determine work aids and sequence of installations. Inspects structure to ascertain obstructions to be avoided to prevent weakening of structure from installation of pipe. Locates and marks position of pipe and pipe connections and passage holes for pipes in walls and floors, using ruler, spirit level, and plumb bob. Cuts openings in walls and floors to accommodate pipe and pipe fittings, using pipe cutters, cutting torch, and pipe threading machine. Bends pipe to required angle by using pipe-bending machine or by placing pipe over block and bending it by hand. Assembles and installs valves, pipe fittings, and pipes composed of metals, such as iron, steel, brass, and lead, and of non-metals, such as glass, vitrified clay, and plastic, using handtools and power tools. Joins pipes by use of screws, bolts, fittings, or solder, and caulks joints. Fills pipe system with water or air and reads pressure gauges to determine whether system is leaking. Installs and repairs plumbing fixtures, such as sinks, commodes, bathtubs, water heater, hot water tanks, garbage disposal units, dishwashers, and water softeners. Repairs and maintains plumbing by replacing washers in leaky faucets, mending burst pipes, and opening clogged drains. May weld holding fixtures to steel structural members.

You now have a complete list of the many operations performed by a plumber. Study this list carefully to determine if all the skills described are necessary or desirable for student employment upon completion of the course and if the time span of the course is sufficient to reasonably expect a student to be able to acquire all of them. In this particular occupation and in several others, it is required that a person work as an apprentice for a given length of time after entry into the trade, regardless of pre-employment training, before being considered a journeyman craftsman. If this is the case it may be unecessary to teach all the skills described in the job description, since the basic skills are adequate to enter employment at the beginner or apprentice level. If there are open-shop employment opportunities, it may be desirable to train to a much higher level of skill, since frequently no period of apprenticeship is needed.

## Step Two

You can easily determine the major skills demanded for any job if you have a comprehensive job description like the one above. You don't even have to know anything about the job. Just pick out the verbs in the job description along with their objects and you have a list of all the important things a person in this occupation is required to do.

Somewhat more difficult is determining the knowledge necessary to perform the "do skills." Here is where you must have the assistance of someone who actually knows how the job is done. Let's perform this procedure on the job description for a plumber given above. We come up with this list of skills:

| | |
|---|---|
| ASSEMBLES<br>INSTALLS<br>REPAIRS | pipes, fittings, fixtures of heating and drainage systems, valves, plumbing fixtures, sinks, commodes, bathtubs, water heaters, water tanks, dish-washers, disposal units, water softeners, etc. |
| STUDIES or<br>READS | blueprints, building plans, specifications. |
| DETERMINES | working aids required and sequence of installation. |

On a 5" x 8" card list on the top line each verb in the job description and below it on the following lines list the object of this verb. For example, referring to the job description above the first verb is "assembles," and the objects of this verb are "pipes, fittings, and fixtures of heating, water, and drainage systems." Your entry on the card would look like this:

ASSEMBLES          pipes, fittings, and fixtures of heating, water and drainage systems.

Another verb in the description is "studies," and the objects are "building plans and working drawings."

Continue until you have listed each verb in the job description with the objects of each. You will now have a comprehensive list of the "do skills" required in this occupation.

## Step Three

Step three is to identify the "know skills." This is more difficult and requires the assistance of someone who knows the occupation well. One factor that must be considered at this point is the basic educational achievement level of the students for whom the course is planned. Too often it is assumed that because a student is in the high school he can adequately apply basic mathematical operations to problem solving and can adequately understand what he reads. This is not necessarily true—even when grades are passing. It is usually necessary to include some of this instruction to assure satisfactory performance. Taking each skill, consider carefully what knowledge a person must have in order to perform it correctly. For example, to correctly assemble pipe one must know the various types, kind, and sizes of pipe and the proper method for joining each. For assembling fittings he must know all the many types of fittings, their proper use, and the correct sealant to be used, if any. Assembly of heating fixtures requires a knowledge of the function, specifications, safety requirements and controls. List item of knowledge on the appropriate card immediately below the "do skills."

The basic job analysis is now complete and you are ready to use it to prepare a course outline.

## PREPARING THE COURSE OUTLINE FROM JOB ANALYSIS

Before starting to prepare the course outline there are certain terms that you must define. Course instruction is divided into major instructional units called "blocks." These blocks are further divided into smaller units called "operations" for "do skills," and "related information" for "know skills." In actual lesson planning and in instruction these smaller units are broken down even further into procedure steps and specific items of knowledge. These blocks are usually arranged in order of instructional sequence from the simple to the more complex and from the most often used to the seldom needed.

Now, using the job analysis cards, arrange them into blocks. A logical organization can be as follows:

Block 1. Safety
Block 2. Basic Tools and Operations
Block 3. Blueprint Reading and Plumbing Code
Block 4. Layout
Block 5. Assembly and Fabrication
Block 6. Installation
Block 7. Repairs
Block 8. Maintenance
Block 9. Testing and Trouble Shooting

After you have grouped the units of instruction into blocks and arranged the blocks in a proper teaching sequence, you are ready to complete the course of study outline. Under each block list each topic in the order in which it should be introduced. As much as possible, each topic should be based on or related to the skills and knowledge previously learned. Your course outline when completed should look something like this:

## COURSE OUTLINE FOR PLUMBING

Block I.    Safety
        A. Standard safety regulations
           1. Eye protection
           2. Protective clothing
           3. Lifting safely
           4. Ladder and scaffold safety
           5. Fire protection
        B. Cutting tool safety
        C. Burn and explosion prevention
           1. Flame control
           2. Explosive gases
           3. Molten metal
           4. Handling hot material
        D. First aid
           1. Cuts and scratches
           2. Burns
           3. Bruises and sprains
           4. Electric shock
Block II.   Basic tools and operations
        A. Use of basic tools
           1. Pipe wrenches
           2. Pipe cutters
           3. Rulers
           4. Level
           5. Square
           6. Plumb bob
           7. Hand taps and dies
           8. Power threading machine
           9. Pipe benders
          10. Cutting tools
              a. Chisels
              b. Saws
              c. Drills
          11. Testing for leaks
          12. Soldering
          13. Welding
          14. Caulking
          15. Valve reseating

## Course Outline for Plumbing (continued)

Block III.   Blueprint reading and plumbing code
  A. Blueprint reading
     1. Alphabet of lines
     2. Piping and plumbing symbols
     3. Standard abbreviations
     4. Scale reading
     5. Freehand sketches as working drawings
  B. Plumbing code
     1. State regulations
     2. Local code
     3. Licensing procedure
     4. Sanitation
     5. Sewage disposal and treatment

Block IV.   Layout
  A. Inspection of structures
  B. Identifying and avoiding obstructions
  C. Locating and marking position of fixtures
  D. Routing piping

Block V.    Assembly and fabrication
  A. Drain stacks
  B. Vent stocks
  C. Heating systems
  D. Water supply systems
  E. Gas supply systems

Block VI.   Installations
  A. Drainage systems
  B. Fixtures
  C. Appliances
  D. Heating systems
  E. Water supply systems
  F. Gas supply systems

Block VII.  Repairs
  A. Leaks in piping systems
  B. Valves in faucets
  C. Replacing controls
  D. Cleaning clogged drains
  E. Miscellaneous repairs

**Course Outline for Plumbing (continued)**

Block VIII. Maintenance
    A. Inspection
    B. Locating lines
      1. Water
      2. Gas
    C. Adjusting of controls
    D. Lubrication
Block IX.   Testing and trouble shooting
    A. Testing piping system
      1. Free flow
      2. Hydrostatic
      3. Compressed air
    B. Test equipment
      1. Gas leak detectors
      2. Metal detectors
      3. Gauges
      4. Pumps
      5. Compressors
    C. Trouble shooting
      1. Systematic testing
      2. Detail observation
      3. Trouble analysis
      4. Solution by elimination of causes
      5. By substitution of components

This course outline is the basis for selecting equipment and designing facilities, and is the nucleus from which the teacher will develop his lesson plans and course of study. No two course outlines for the same vocational course will be the same if prepared for two different schools by different people; however, they will be similar to the one we have produced.

## HOW TO DETERMINE FACILITIES AND EQUIPMENT REQUIRED

By this time you know what is to be taught, and approximately how. What are you going to need to teach with?

What kind and how large a room will be required? With the aid of the subject matter specialist you can find this from the course outline just completed. Let's take a look at this outline. The first block is on safety and Section "A" is on safety regulations. This refers to the regulations established by law and also by custom in many occupations. A handbook published by OSHA that covers all legally mandated rules may be obtained from the Department of Labor Safety. Preferably each student should have his own copy.

On a sheet of paper headed "Instructional Material" write "OSHA Manual." The first unit under Section A is "Eye protection." The manual will contain the information on how to use these items and why, and since we must use these protectors we must include them in the equipment list. For eye protection in a plumbing class you will need three kinds of goggles or eye shields: clear goggles for grinding or chipping, etc., dark welding goggles for gas welding and brazing, and hoods or face shields if electric welding is taught, as is usually the case. Sanitary regulations require that each student have his own or that the school provide a means of sterilization between use by different persons. On a second piece of paper, headed "Tools and Equipment," list the three kinds of goggles and shields.

As you go through the outline some items will be obvious even to those who know little about the occupation, but many must be identified by someone who is experienced in the trade. A good example of the discrimination in equipment selection can be seen in unit four. Most shops should have a ladder, but many will not require a scaffold. This will depend on the types of construction projects planned.

When the equipment list has been prepared, you are ready to determine the type and size of the physical facility needed. Using the dimensions of each piece of fixed equipment you can determine the installation space required. Care must be taken to assure that each machine has adequate clearance, and that work space is arranged so that its operation does not create a safety hazard for those at adjacent work stations. Other factors that must be considered are storage space, related instructional area, traffic flow between work stations, lighting, in some shop courses exhaust and ventilation, and student load.

If the teacher has been selected to teach the course he should be consulted on the selection of all equipment. If the teacher is unknown, a qualified person from prospective employers can help the administrator select the proper equipment. In many cases such aid is available from the state education department in the form of a recommended list of equipment for specific courses, or they will have a consultant who can help determine equipment needs.

# 3

# Funding
# the Vocational Education
# Program

**CHAPTER 3**  Adequate funding of vocational education is essential to development of an effective program. For a few of the more affluent school systems this is not a problem, since there are sufficient funds available. For most schools, however, funds must be obtained from other sources to help defray the additional cost of equipment, facilities and instructional supplies required for vocational education.

## FINDING FUNDING SOURCES

One of the responsibilities of the vocational administrator is to locate a source for these funds and take the necessary action to obtain them. As you shall see, there are various techniques and strategies for solving this problem. The most common source of funds other than local tax money is the State Department of Education. These funds are usually a combination of state and federal money appropriated for occupational education and may be used only for specified purposes and only in accordance with certain regulations. It is one of the cardinal facts of educational funding that any money obtained from any source will have some restrictions and guidelines for its use. The administrator should carefully consider these use controls, the effect they will have on the planned program, the extent of other than local control of the educational program and its effect, and also the supervision, evaluation and reporting required. Sometimes extremely rigid, narrow restrictions and onerous, frequent, and detailed reporting may so adversely affect the program as to make funding from such a source unadvisable. Most guideline regulations, however, are intended to assure a quality program and prevent abuse and misuse of funds. In any case, if the program cannot be adapted to the funding restrictions without seriously impairing the effectiveness of the instruction, other funding should be sought.

The State Department of Education should be the first funding source investigated and usually requires the simplest application for fund allocation. Some kinds of occupational education programs may be funded directly from the U.S. Office of Education through a grant to the local education agency. These grants are most often for pilot programs employing new and innovative instructional methods and/or materials, to determine their effectiveness. The procedures for obtaining these grants can often be complex and tedious, involving the preparation of a detailed formal proposal in accordance with very specific guideline stipulations. Extensive evaluation of programs and effectiveness and frequent reporting, including detailed fiscal records, are usually requested.

Funds received from the state are most frequently a mixture of state and federal funds. Though these funds may vary from state to state depending upon the State Plan for Vocational Education, most states include teacher's salary for regular programs, partial or complete equipment funds for new programs, and in some cases funds for updating and improving ongoing programs. It is possible under some circumstances to obtain state assistance in construction of facilities. Funds for development and implementation of pilot programs through the state from federal allocations may be obtained. Sometimes there is also an allowance for supplies.

Private foundations often provide funds for certain educational activities in which they have a particular interest and which they believe enhance and promote the objectives of the foundations. The range of educational interest among private foundations is great, and though they are a relatively minor source of support, it is advisable to investigate the feasibility of such funding for programs which are closely related to the purposes of such foundations.

A source of funding for occupational education that is becoming increasingly important is industry. Many of the larger organizations are becoming aware of the importance of the schools in promoting such programs as they believe will provide them with a source of skill-trained, better prepared, entry-level workers. Some industries are researching the effect of occupational education in the schools on the training required for entry-level workers to determine the advantage and feasibility of supporting such education. The automotive industry, one of the pioneers in this effort, provides many educational aids and in some cases financial support for programs designed to direct and develop qualified students toward a career in the automotive field. Industry support of occupational education is not limited to national industrial complexes. Sometimes a local business organization will provide support and financial aid to the local school for an educational program designed to develop skill-trained students as a continuing source of employees for jobs in their organization.

Two examples of such support from specific industries come readily to mind. A clothing manufacturing company or group of companies may need power sewing machine operators and may be willing to provide the use of equipment, supplies, sometimes the facilities, and a source of instructional personnel to a local school to induce them to set up such a program. Usually these companies will assure employment for all who successfully complete the training.

Another example is a shipyard or an oil company that has a continuing need for welders. Sometimes they will assist the school with equipment and other costs in order to assure a continuing source of welders trained to their special needs.

Now that we have discussed possible funding sources, let's see how you can locate the one most appropriate to your needs. Ask yourself some questions about the planned program. Is it a usual type of program normally a part of public school programs in your area? If so, it is likely that funding is readily available from the State Department of Education. Is the planned course designed to meet a new educational need? Do you plan to use new and different instructional methods? Is the proposed course designed for those students who have special needs not being satisfied by the present program? If the answer to one or more of these questions is "yes," you will probably qualify for a grant either through the State Department, from the U.S. Office of Education, or through a prime sponsor of revenue-sharing projects in your area. Is the course designed to meet a specific local occupational need for workers? If so, it has probably been planned in cooperation with the organizations who need the employees, and they can be a logical source of support. Does the prepared program closely relate to the objectives of a private foundation? If you believe it does, you may want to inquire if the foundation offers aid or support through free instructional supplies or other means.

As previously mentioned, the State Education Agency is usually the first source to which you will turn for financing. A letter, phone call or visit will usually bring immediate information concerning funding available and often the State Agency will provide a consultant to work with you in preparing the application. In most cases these state education officials are anxious to assist you to develop the best vocational program for your local needs, and if funding is not available for the proposed program through their regular funding procedure, it may be through some special division such as Research and Development or through the Department's discretionary fund program. If there is no provision for aid from the state agency, often the consultant can suggest where funds may be available.

The Federal Government publishes a guide to federal aid to education which may be obtained from the Superintendent of Documents or at most public libraries. This publication lists all the various federal agencies that provide financial assistance to public schools and a description of the types of programs each is designed to promote, with instructions for obtaining more detailed information on those that seem to be probable sources. Most public libraries have a file of all the larger foundations that support educational, cultural, and vocational courses. Most of these foundations are eager to provide information concerning their objectives and are willing to discuss your proposal if it seems to be particularly relevant to the cause espoused by the organization. When you have decided on the source of funding, you are ready to make application.

## HOW TO USE GUIDELINES
## FOR PROPOSAL PREPARATION

If you are applying to the State Department for allocation of a regular vocational program, you have a relatively simple task in preparing the application. Most agencies have standardized forms to be completed with factual and statistical information. These will be furnished to you upon request along with instructions for completing them. If your proposed program is to be funded as a pilot or research project, the application usually requires a proposal which states clearly the purpose of the project and describes the objectives and the proposed manner of accomplishing them. Each of the various funding agencies has its own set of guidelines which describe the required format of a proposal. These guides vary a great deal in specifications and details, some being much more complex and rigid than others. However, most have general requirements that are common to all. Let's discuss briefly the components of a proposal for a pilot occupational program.

### Title Page

This is usually the first page and contains a title that is descriptive of the planned program.

## Abstract

The title page is usually followed by the abstract—a brief, concise statement of the purpose of the proposal program and what it is expected to accomplish. Many times the length of the abstract is strictly limited to a single paragraph or page, sometimes to a certain number of words or characters. Because of this brevity the writing of an abstract requires very careful structure and choice of words. A poorly written abstract can jeopardize the favorable consideration of the proposal.

## Statement of Need or Statement of Problem

This statement indicates the need to be met or the problem to be solved by the proposed program. The description should be specific and detailed enough to clearly identify the need or problem and why it must be satisfied or solved.

## Statement of Objectives

List a set of specific measurable objectives. Objectives may be stated in terms of what the students will be able to do measurably differently as a result of the course.

## Number and Type of Participants

Students should be identified as to grade level, numbers, ethnic or socio-economic breakdown, etc.

## Description of Activities

This part tells what is to be done, when, and how. The activities should directly reflect the needs or problems described in the statement of the needs and should indicate the means for attaining the objectives. The organization of the project, a tentative schedule of classes, the number of requested teacher units, and a brief description of how the project will be conducted should be included.

A tentative course outline, and, when possible, the materials the instructor will use should be included.

## Qualifications of Personnel

Teachers shall be certified in accordance with the state requirements.

## Facilities and Equipment

The existing facilities that will be used for instruction should be described. Equipment necessary for the instructional program should be described and an itemized equipment list should be attached.

## Evaluation

Submit a design for evaluation or a plan of evaluation. The evaluation should include provision for follow-up of students. In addition to the local evaluation, a state evaluation may be conducted.

## Budget

Prepare the budget in the format specified.

The following proposal is a sample of the type described.


PROPOSAL FOR EXEMPLARY BUSINESS
OCCUPATIONS LABORATORY

Submitted to the Division of Occupational Research and Development
Department of Occupational and Technical Education
Texas Education Agency

TITLE OF PROPOSED PROJECT:    Middle School Exploratory
                              Business Occupations
                              Laboratory

APPLICANT ORGANIZATION:       Harlandale Independent
                              School Dist.
                              102 Genevieve,
                              San Antonio, Texas 78285

PROPOSAL DEVELOPED BY:
                              _____
                              Wm. H. Bentley, Director
                              Vocational Education,
                              512-924-2301

PROPOSAL TRANSMITTED BY:

Wm. H. Bentley, Director
Vocational Education,
512-924-2301

CONTRACTING OFFICER

C. N. Boggess,
Superintendent
Harlandale Independent
School Dist. 512-924-2301

DURATION OF PROJECT:          July 1, 19-- to June 30, 19--
TOTAL EXPENDITURES REQUIRED
   FOR PROPOSED PROJECT:      $12,473.00
DATE TRANSMITTED:             April 30, 19--

---

### FLY LEAF
1. This proposal has not been submitted to any other agency or organization.
2. No similar proposal for a Middle School Exploratory Business Occupations Laboratory has been previously submitted.
3. This proposal is a redirection of a consultant unit to an exploratory unit.
4. The applicant is a local educational agency.

---

## ABSTRACT

The proposed project has been developed to meet a specific need at one of our middle schools. In this school the student population is composed almost entirely of Spanish-surnamed pupils from the lower economic group. There are many potential dropouts, over-aged for grade (15-17 in grade 8), frustrated and discouraged, with little motivation to continue high school education. An exploratory laboratory in business related occupations will do much to make these students aware of their potential and let them determine an occupational choice. Thus they will not only be motivated to continue in high school in order to prepare for employment but will have a basis for choosing their occupation and planning their educational program.

The objectives of this program are as follows:

1. To provide an opportunity for pupils to experience firsthand the activities of many business-related occupations.
2. To let each student determine for himself those activities that he likes and can successfully learn to perform.
3. To stimulate an interest in continuing in high school.
4. To provide some basic skill and useful practical knowledge of the business world.

It is expected that this course will effectively alleviate the dropout problem for those who participate and will encourage them to prepare for future employment.

**Problem:**

In one of the Harlandale middle schools, located in a low income neighborhood, the student body is composed almost entirely of Spanish-surnamed pupils. Many of them are over-aged for their grade level, due mostly to learning difficulties in the first school years because of language deficiencies and lack of cultural background conducive to educational achievement. Consequently, there are many in the eighth grade who are 15 to 18 years old, frustrated, discouraged, who see little need for staying in school or going on to high school. Unless these students are helped to understand that they can learn skills that will enable them to be employed after graduation, most of them will leave school, obtaining only the lowest paid jobs or getting married and living on welfare.

**Description:**

The Business Occupations Exploratory Course is a laboratory type program in which the student actually uses the equipment and performs the procedures, thus through hands-on experience gains insight as to his interests and aptitudes. The class is conducted one 55-minute period per day for one year. The topics covered will include the following: use of many common business machines, such as typewriter, adding machine, cash register, mimeograph, duplicator, etc.; practice in business procedures, such as filing, record keeping, inventory, ordering, sales display, sales presentation, advertising, etc. By operating the office machines, keeping records, filing, and practicing other business procedures, each

student will understand his interests and will be able to determine
for himself if he has the aptitude for a business career.

**Objectives:**
1. Provide an opportunity for pupils to experience firsthand the
   activities of many business-related occupations.
2. Help each student determine for himself those activities which
   he likes and which he has the ability to successfully learn.
3. Stimulate an interest in continuing in school.
4. Provide some basic skill and useful practical knowledge of the
   business world and its various occupations.

**Administration:**
   This program will be administered under the direction of the
Assistant Administrator for Occupational Education and
Technology, through the principal. Supervision will be by the
principal and by the Vocational Supervisor.

**Procedures:**
   *A. General Design:* This project is designed to motivate potential
dropouts to continue in school by helping them develop an understanding of their interests and capabilities and of the many
opportunities open to them through educational preparation.
Hands-on laboratory experiences are provided so that each student
can practice doing those activities common to business occupations
to determine suitability for this kind of career. For those students
who desire to enter preparation for a business occupation, a general
business introductory course will be provided at the ninth grade level
so that there will be no interruption in occupational training from
the eighth grade through graduation.
   *B. Schools:* The only school to participate under this proposal will
be Leal Middle School.
   *C. Participants:* Participants will be students of the eighth grade
who are interested in determining whether they are suited for a
business career. Preference in recruitment will be given those who
are one or more years over-aged for grade level. Both boys and girls
will be eligible; however, it is anticipated that the large majority of
students selecting this course will be girls.
   *D. Methods and materials:* There is believed to be adequate
instructional material available that can be adapted to use in this

course. Material will be developed if necessary to meet recognized needs. Methods will be adapted to meet the particular requirements of exploration of this grade level.

*E. Evaluation:* Evaluation will consist of two phases. Continuous evaluation will be based on observation, reports of teacher, counselors, supervisors, principal, pupils and parents. Long-term evaluation of program effectiveness can be readily determined by comparison of the dropout rate of those pupils enrolled in this course with their classmates and by the ratio of success to failure for those who continue in business preparatory courses, compared to those who did not have this experience.

*F. Time schedule:* Actual time schedule will extend for ten months throughout the school year.

### Coordination and Dissemination:

This program will be coordinated with other instructional activities so as to avoid duplication of effort. The subject matter will be coordinated with the business preparatory offering of the high school so that transition to the high school course will provide uninterrupted educational progress. Any materials developed will be available for examination by other educational institutions, public and private. The Texas Education Agency will be provided with copies of all material for reproduction and distribution upon request. Other interested educators will be welcome to observe the methods used upon request.

### Personnel:

The teacher of this course will meet all certification and approval qualifications as defined by the Texas State Plan for Vocational Education and by the Texas Education Agency.

### Facilities:

Adequate classroom facilities are available at the school for which this program is proposed.

### Special Funding Provision:

Adequate accounting will be employed to avoid commingling of funds in such a way that identity is lost. Auditability of all expenditures is assured.

Budget Sheet

Program:   Exploratory Business Occupations Laboratory

Applicant
Organization:   Harlandale Independent School District

TEA Use Only
Project No. _____

Co. Dist. No.    015-904

FINANCIAL PLAN

Effective Dates:    July 1, 19-- to    June 30, 19--

| Column (1) Items | (2) Applicant's Budget Account No. | (3) Estimated Expenditures[1] |
|---|---|---|
| A.   Salaries and Wages[2] | | 9470.00 |
| B.   Fringe Benefits | | |
| C.   Travel | | 300.00 |
| D.   Supplies[3] | | |
| E.   Teaching Aids[3] | | |
| F.   Equipment[3] | | |
| G.   Other Costs: | | |
| (1) _____ | | 2703.00 |
| (2) _____ | | |
| (3) _____ | | |
| (4) _____ | | |
| (5) _____ | | |
| (6) _____ | | |
| (7) _____ | | |
| TOTAL EXPENDITURES /1 | | $12,473.00 |

| TEA Use Only | | |
|---|---|---|
| Local Funds | | |
| State Vocational Funds | | |
| State's Share of Cost | | _____ % |

---

[1]Means the amount of funds (Federal, State, local) approved by the Texas
Education Agency for designated services, materials, and other items.
[2]Personnel plan is required—See Attachment I.
[3]Supply and equipment lists are required.

FINANCIAL PLAN—ATTACHMENT I

Applicant
Organization: Harlandale Independent School District

| Vocational Personnel Plan | | | | | |
|---|---|---|---|---|---|
| A. Vocational Salaries and Wages: Give name and position title. | 1 % of Time on Project (Check one) | | (1) No. of Months Employed | (2) Monthly Salary | (3) Base Salary |
| | Full Time | Half Time | | | |
| 1. Carolyn Jean Reakes   Teacher | X | | 10  X | 947  = | 9470 |
| 2. | | | X | = | |
| 3. | | | X | = | |
| 4. | | | X | = | |
| 5. | | | X | = | |
| 6. | | | X | = | |
| 7. | | | X | = | |
| 8. | | | X | = | |
| 9. | | | X | = | |
| 10. | | | X | = | |
| | | | | TOTAL: | 9470 |

| B. Travel: List by position title. | |
|---|---|
| 1.   Teacher | $  300 |
| 2. | |
| 3. | |
| 4. | |
| 5. | |
| 6. | |
| 7. | |
| 8. | |
| 9. | |
| 10. | |
| TOTAL: | $  300 |

EQUIPMENT LIST

| | | |
|---|---|---:|
| 5 | Manual Typewriters @ $150 | $  750.00 |
| 3 | Adding Machines @ 119 | 357.00 |
| 1 | Electric Printing Calculator @ 349 | 349.00 |
| 1 | Stencil A. B. Dick 325 $325 | 325.00 |
| 1 | Spirit A. B. Dick 210 $300 | 300.00 |
| 2 | File Cabinets @ $60.75 | 121.50 |
| 1 | Cash Register reconditioned | 500.00 |
| | | $2702.50 |

# 4

# Recruiting
# and Training
# Vocational Personnel

**CHAPTER 4** After all the planning is done and the funding is procured comes probably the most important responsibility of the vocational administrator—recruiting and selecting teachers. The most elaborate facility, the finest equipment, abundant supplies and interested students cannot provide effective occupational education without the leadership of a qualified, dedicated teacher.

Vocational teachers are generally much more difficult to recruit and employ than academic teachers. Reason for this are the strict qualifications required for certification of vocational teachers and the low salary schedule compared to the salary they can earn in business and industrial jobs.

## LOCATING TEACHERS

Two of the oldest vocational courses, Vocational Agriculture and Vocational Homemaking, require teachers specifically prepared in a college or university approved for vocational teacher education in these areas. The qualifications for these teachers are similar in all the states. Teachers in these fields can be recruited in the same way as academic teachers—from the ranks of experienced teachers or through the teacher placement office of the college or university.

Qualifications for teachers of business and clerical courses, while requiring a college degree in the subject field, usually also require one to five years of actual working experience in the occupation for which training is given. The two principal sources for teachers in these two categories are as follows: (1) experienced teachers who have occupational experience prior to entering the teaching profession, and (2) persons employed in clerical or business occupations who desire to enter teaching. Many of this group will require additional courses in educational methods to meet full certification requirements. The most difficult teachers to find are those for skilled occupations in industry. Very few institutions of higher learning offer preparatory education for teachers of industrial education. Usually such skilled craftsmen have technical degrees or none at all. Many have only experience or apprentice training. Where, then, can you find persons qualified to teach vocational industrial courses? You must look for them where they are—employed in industry.

## SECURING APPLICATIONS

Several methods have been successfully used to secure applications for vocational teacher employment.

1. Publicize the need among your fellow educators and ask their recommendations of any qualified friend or acquaintance who may be interested.
2. The State Education Agency often can supply a list of applicants who have been approved for teaching permits or certification.
3. Vocational teachers in the same occupational field often have a wide acquaintance with other teachers or craftsmen who are interested in becoming vocational teachers.

4. Advertisement in newspapers is sometimes used effectively.
5. Teacher placement agencies are sometimes used satisfactorily if adequate counseling and screening are done.

## SCREENING AND QUALIFYING APPLICANTS

Interviewing and selecting the best teacher from the applicants often poses a puzzling problem, especially for the administrator who has little knowledge of the occupation for which he seeks a teacher. One of the preliminary steps which is frequently part of the application process is a "Statement of Qualifications," or comprehensive resume of the applicant's past employment and education experience. Most states require that such a statement be submitted to the central education agency for evaluation and approval prior to issuing a permit or certificate.

The information given in this resume can provide many clues to the applicant's characteristics if carefully analyzed. Some of the factors to consider are as follows:

1. How many years of work experience does he have in this field? Though the length of experience does not necessarily insure that an applicant is an expert craftsman, it does indicate that he has been able to function adequately in the occupation. This factor has to be considered in conjunction with the next four factors.

2. Is work experience adequately described? A detailed description of the specific work experiences is necessary in order to assess the probable skill of the applicant. If such adequate description is not included in the application form it should be determined in the interview.

3. Has applicant completed technical training courses? Completion of such courses indicates an effort to improve occupational skill and competence. A good teacher must be willing to continuously update technical and teaching skills. A history of

completion of training and study in the past can be interpreted as an indication of his willingness to complete the necessary workshops and conferences that will be required of him as a teacher.

4. Are references given for technical competence employers or supervisors for whom he has worked? These persons are usually best able to accurately assess his technical competence.

5. How recent is his trade experience? In this time of rapidly developing technology a person may have had many years of experience and still be inadequate in technical competence if the experience is not reasonably recent.

6. How adequate is the applicant's education background? It is important that he have communicational and computational ability adequate for the occupation to be taught. Though educational background cannot assure such ability, it may provide some clues.

7. How frequently has the applicant changed jobs? Why? This can be a very important clue to the person who lacks either occupational skill or the ability to get along with his fellow workers or employers. Sometimes he is just a drifter who does not stay long on any job. The *why* is very important, and in cases of frequent job changes this should be investigated before employment.

8. Is the handwriting legible? Though granted that many teachers have poor penmanship, the ability to write or print legibly on a chalkboard is important to most teaching situations.

9. If narrative format is used, are sentence structure and punctuation correct for clarity of expression? If not, this can cause a considerable problem in communication in cases where much of the information is given in teacher-prepared material.

10. Is the form filled out properly, neatly, and completely? This can be an indicator of the applicant's ability to understand written instructions, neatness, and carelessness.

Interviewing prospective vocational teachers follows the usual pattern of employment interviews. However, since the purpose of the interview is to determine the applicant's suitability for the job to be done, it is somewhat more difficult for many educators for two reasons. First, assessment of technical competence in an unfamiliar field is very hard to do. Second, certain personal characteristics which are desirable for all teachers are *essential* for teaching skills. Such teachers must not only be thoroughly skill-competent but must also be able to guide the student as he acquires this skill. Such teaching demands great patience, since many trials and failures accompany skill development. The teacher must be able to help the student avoid loss of interest through the discouragement of failure. Teaching skill-development laboratory courses demands organizational and managerial ability far beyond that required for classroom teaching of academic subjects. Effective preparation for employment must include affective learning as well as cognitive and psychomotor learning. Therefore the vocational teacher must not only have a thorough knowledge of the technology and be skilled in the performance of all the many skills to be taught, but must also have the ability to stimulate and develop in the student the attitudes and behavior habits necessary for success in his career. Some of the questions which can help in assessing the probable effectiveness of the vocational teacher who has had no past teaching experience are listed here:

1. Why do you want to teach?
2. Have you been happy in your job?
3. What experiences have you had in working with youth?
4. In what organizations are you active?
5. What experience have you had in teaching others to do things and in explaining how things work?
6. What do you see as the most important problem in today's society?
7. Are you willing to acquire additional specific education courses and in-service training to improve your ability to teach?

## ORIENTATION OF NEW VOCATIONAL TEACHERS

Anyone entering into employment needs certain information concerning his responsibilities and the rules by which he is to play his role. Orientation for experienced teachers, newly employed, may consist of little more than a handbook of local policies. Others just entering the teaching profession or from other states should have more instruction in what is expected of them. This is particularly true for the person who has never taught and who has had no formal educational preparation for teaching. These beginning teachers need all the information and assistance the administrator can provide if they are to develop maximum effectiveness in the shortest period of time.

The following points must be covered in orientation:

1. The exact duties the teacher is expected to perform.
2. Local policies.
3. State regulations.
4. Methods and techniques for effective instruction.
5. Discipline policies and approved disciplinary procedures.
6. How to keep necessary records.
7. Grading systems.
8. From whom to obtain additional information when needed.
9. By what criteria his performance will be evaluated.

## 1. The Exact Duties the Teacher Is to Perform

Every employee is entitled to know exactly what is expected of him, and vocational teachers are no exception. The following is a job description that lists each important function of the vocational teacher:

A. Shall interview prospective students to explain the instructional program and to determine their interest and potential to profit from the training. He will work closely with the vocational counselor in screening and selection of students.

B. Shall plan, organize, and conduct an instructional program designed to develop vocational skills, technical knowledge, and work habits in accordance with a course of study based on analysis of the occupation taught which includes the skills and knowledge necessary for success in the occupation.

C. Shall work closely with the local advisory committee in planning the training to meet the changing demands of industry. He shall update the instructional procedure to include new technological practice and knowledge. Major changes in the instructional program should be discussed with and approved by the vocational administrator.

D. Shall prepare and maintain lesson plans and other instructional material in accordance with the recommendations of the State Education Agency and local administrators. Assistance will be given new teachers, who need it, in learning to prepare this material. (Samples of lesson plans, instruction sheets, operation sheets, job sheets, and tests are provided in this book and may be adapted to meet the needs of a local program if desired.)

E. Shall insure safety in those courses which are hazardous by:

(1) Regular organized instruction in safe practice.
(2) Maintaining tools and equipment in safe condition.
(3) Use of safety devices.
(4) Formulating and enforcing safety rules.
(5) Reporting any hazard which he cannot immediately correct to the principal and to the vocational supervisor.

F. Shall maintain accurate records of student's progress, identifying the skills and knowledge in which he is proficient.

## 2. Local Policies

Every school has certain policies established by the school board and/or by administration which are designed for the requirements of that particular school. These policies vary greatly from district to district, and even more from state to state. A teacher coming into the school either from another school or direct from industry should be given a copy of local policies. (An example of a policy statement is presented here.)

A. Shall cooperate with vocational counselors, local employment agencies and employers in providing such data and information concerning each student's abilities as may be needed in occupational placement of those completing the program.

B. Shall comply with recommendations of State Education Agency and local administrator in formulating and implementing a check-out procedure for tools in courses in which tools are used. He shall report all broken, worn out, lost, or stolen tools and equipment to the vocational supervisor.

C. Shall supervise and coordinate work experience of students when such work experience is an integral part of the planned training program.

D. Shall provide leadership, direction, promotion, and supervision for the vocational youth organizations provided for the program taught.

E. Shall maintain an accurate inventory of all equipment, tools, supplies, and materials under his control and make periodic reports of such inventory to the vocational director.

F. Shall requisition instruction material in accordance with local school policy.

G. Shall keep accurate record of material used in making repairs and/or building articles for the personal benefit of students and others. All material so used shall be charged for and the money receipted and deposited with the designated school official for credit to his program budget.

H. Shall maintain follow-up records on all students and report the data as requested by the vocational counselor and supervisor.

I. Shall complete and submit all required reports properly and when due.

## 3. State Regulations

State regulations vary greatly from state to state. In most states there are written program standards for each vocational course. The new teacher should be provided with a copy of these standards and should have them explained to him. Since state standards are sometimes recommendations, optional for the local district, any deviation from the written standards by local policy should be clearly explained.

## 4. Methods and Techniques for Effective Instruction

There are many methods of instruction. Some are more appropriate for use in certain types of vocational courses than in others. For example, in a welding course, demonstration and student practice are usually more effective, while in a part-time cooperative type course where students are employed part-time away from school, classroom instruction is more frequently individual assignment and directed study of related technical material. Each teacher will develop his own peculiar ways of using each method. But for the sake of new teachers we will discuss a few of the most common practices in vocational instruction.

A. *Lecture* is probably the most used and the least effective of all methods of instruction. Many teachers consider it the easiest method for conducting a class. However, as one of my professors often said, "Telling is not teaching." It takes an expert lecturer to present such a vivid and interesting talk that it will attract and hold the attention of the listeners so well that they learn and retain information given by this method.

B. There is a Chinese proverb that describes a picture as being worth a thousand words. The use of pictures such as films, transparencies, posters, diagrams, etc., is one of the more effective instructional devices. Since pictures are usually accompanied with verbal discussion and explanation, this method is usually called audio-visual.

C. *Demonstration* is an important instructional tool. The teacher shows exactly how an operation is performed, explaining each step carefully and answering all questions. This method is particularly useful in teaching manipulative skills.

D. *Student practice* is the means by which most learning is accomplished. Unless the student becomes involved in the actual performance he usually learns little. This is equally true whether the learner is being taught to operate a lathe, write a letter, or make a sales presentation.

E. *Simulation and role-playing* techniques are often used when it is not possible or feasible to practice in an actual live situation. This method, which can be very effective when properly designed and conducted, requires a great deal of preparation, planning and practice on the part of the teacher to acquire proficiency in its use.

There are many other teaching strategies used that cannot be discussed here. Each teacher will, with experience, develop a pattern of instruction peculiar to him. Innovation by teachers is the way new techniques are developed.

## 5. Discipline Policies and Approved Disciplinary Procedures

Without discipline effective learning is not possible. The ideal discipline is self-discipline, where each one controls his own behavior in a proper manner. It is the responsibility of the teacher to help each student develop this ability. To accomplish this, certain rules of conduct and control are necessary. The general principles of disciplinary policy are included in local policies or mandated by law. However, in many school districts each campus has its own set of approved procedures for handling disciplinary problems. These are usually included in a teacher's handbook or guide. Each new teacher should be provided with one for the school in which he is to teach. This should be discussed and explained during orientation of new teachers.

## 6. How to Keep Necessary Records

The records that vocational teachers are required to keep vary from state to state, school to school, and sometimes from campus to campus. All teachers must keep a class record book in which they record the names of the class members, attendance record, and usually the grade record of each student.

## 7. Grading Systems

These may be of many types. Most schools have a uniform grading system using either a percentage or letter system; others use only a pass/fail system. A few schools are ungraded. Whatever system is used should be thoroughly explained since many involve subjective evaluation by the teacher. Vocational programs often have special grading systems, such as progress charts, etc.

## 8. From Whom to Obtain Additional Information When Needed

Many times a new teacher will need to ask for information that he has not been given, has forgotten, or does not understand. The type of information needed largely determines who would be most able and available to supply it. If the question concerns the usual procedures of the school, the nearest experienced teacher is usually both able and willing to answer the question. If it is an unusual situation on classroom procedure, the principal or assistant principal may be the only reliable source. If the question concerns vocational regulations, the department head, another vocational teacher, or the vocational supervisor is often the most logical choice. In large systems with several vocational units on each campus, often the "big brother or sister" method is used by assigning an experienced teacher to help a new teacher become adjusted to the program. Most teachers are willing to assist in this manner if requested to do so by the principal, vocational director or superintendent.

### 9. By What Criteria His Performance Will Be Evaluated

Each teacher is entitled to know by what criteria he will be evaluated. The principal criteria used by the author for teacher evaluation are listed here.

A. Ability to plan and conduct instruction.
B. Class organization and control.
C. Observation of student participation and performance.
D. Rapport with students and other staff members.
E. Willingness to accept constructive criticism and try to improve his performance.
F. Degree of success achieved by students trained by him when employed in the occupation.
G. Evaluation report of supervisor and principal.

## PROCEDURES FOR EFFECTIVE ORIENTATION

The procedures for effective orientation can be outlined in specific steps.

1. Provide the teacher with a summary fact booklet which covers the following:
   A. Background of the school.
   B. Overview of the vocational program.
   C. Organization plan for administration and instruction.
   D. Brief digest of local policies.
   E. Schedule of records and reports required.
2. Discuss and explain thoroughly the objectives of the course to be taught.
3. Conduct new teacher on a tour of the campus and introduce him to other teachers in his department.
4. Answer any questions he has.
5. Arrange for an experienced and cooperative teacher in his department to answer the day-to-day questions as they arise and assist him in adjusting to the new position.

## HOW TO PLAN AND CONDUCT IN-SERVICE TRAINING

Most state education departments have developed an extensive in-service program for each vocational education division. This consists of special seminar and evening classes offered by teacher training institutions, usually with college credit. Also included are periodic one- or two-day conferences during the school year and in most cases an annual workshop prior to the beginning of each school year. While these programs are helpful and meet a need for keeping abreast of new developments, they do not deal directly with problems encountered at the local school level.

It is necessary, therefore, that each local school develop and conduct its own program based on the needs and problems of local concern. Though the vocational administrator has the ultimate responsibility for providing the in-service program, he cannot do it alone. Any effective program must be a cooperative effort among administrators, principal, supervisors and teachers.

The first step in planning an in-service program is to assess the needs and problems that need to be met. There are several ways in which this assessment can be accomplished. A survey questionnaire may be prepared for each of the teachers, principals, supervisors, and administrators to determine what they believe is needed and the relative priority of each.

Meet with the entire group to plan the mechanics of conducting the program. In a school large enough to have department heads in each vocational area or on each campus, encourage these persons to provide the leadership in specific program planning of their departments. Arrange for regular meetings scheduled to use released teaching time as much as possible. After the topics are determined, obtain the best qualified person available to conduct each conference or session. Evaluate each meeting with feedback from the participants to determine the effectiveness and identify any revision that may be needed.

The suggestions and procedures described in this chapter, while they have proven effective for the author, are not the only methods that can be used. Each administrator, as he gains experience in recruiting and employing vocational teachers, will find that certain techniques and procedures work more successfully for him than others. He will gradually develop a selection and training system uniquely designed for the schools under his administration. The practices described here can serve as the base for building the system.

# 5

## How to Implement Vocational Programs

**CHAPTER** One of the most important responsibilities of the

**5** administrator of vocational education is implementing new units of occupational training. There are many seemingly minor details that are, however, essential to the successful start of a new program and for continuing effectiveness. The proper facility must be provided; equipment must be selected, purchased and installed; supplies must be procured; and finally students must be carefully selected. These are the problems discussed in this chapter.

## PREPARING THE FACILITIES

Preparing facilities may range from planning and constructing a new building designed to the specific requirements of a particular course, to merely locating and assigning an already existing classroom. In many cases existing facilities may be remodeled adequately and economically.

Early in the planning stage it should have been determined if a suitable building exists, or if construction is required. If construction is necessary, planning should start as soon as the decision has been made to institute the program. In planning the construction or the remodeling of a building to house occupational training classes, most administrators must rely on the expertise of others more knowledgeable of the specific requirements for the occupation for which training is to be conducted.

If the teacher has been selected he should be asked to recommend specific characteristics needed to provide the most effective learning experiences. It is a good idea also to ask someone—or preferably several persons— operating successfully in the occupation to advise in the planning of both the building and the equipment. This will help assure that the training environment simulates closely that found in industry or business. It is also advisable for the administrator to visit industry to see first hand the facilities and equipment commonly used. After it has been determined what special features are needed, the school architect is asked to prepare preliminary plans and cost estimates. These plans are then presented to the school board of trustees, or other governing authority, for approval.

When final plans have been approved, the usual procedure, required by law in many states, is to obtain at least three bids on construction or major remodeling. Bid specifications should be very carefully drawn and bids inspected closely to see that all specifications and conditions are met. This is usually the responsibility of the school architect, but in some cases it is done by the administrator. For some vocational courses a regular classroom is adequate, with little or no alteration, when proper equipment is added. Most State Departments of Education have planning guides for both facilities and equipment, with certain program standards which must be met for program approval and funding. These guides should always be obtained and considered to assure an acceptable program. Several excellent guides are also available from other sources.[1]

---

[1]Texas A & M University and Ohio State University both have vocational planning guides, as do most vocational teacher training institutions. An excellent guide is available from *School Shop Magazine,* Ann Arbor, Michigan.

## PURCHASING AND INSTALLING EQUIPMENT

Proper equipment is as important as the housing, and in some cases more essential to an effective program. The equipment for an occupational course should, as nearly as possible, closely approximate that used in industry, though in some cases additional modification of instructional equipment may make teaching easier and more effective. Again the administrator must rely on advice from those with knowledge of equipment needs for the occupational education being implemented.

The first step is to determine which equipment is essential, which is very desirable, and which would provide enrichment, though not essential to the basic training. The kinds and types of equipment and the number of each required, in most cases when equipment is machines, must be decided prior to planning of the facilities, so that proper space and installation needs can be satisfied.

The second step is to prepare the specifications for bids. These specifications should be very specific and detailed to assure satisfactory quality. It is possible, however, to be so specific and so detailed that only one manufacturer can meet the specifications, thus limiting the number of bidders. This strategy is sometimes used when the administrator wants only one brand or model of an item with no substitution acceptable. In the writer's opinion, whenever several makes or models of machines are approximately equal in major respects, it is preferable that the words "or equal" be included in the bid specifications. Shown here are several sample equipment specifications:

- 2 each, typewriters, manual, pica type, 15" carriage, single key tabulator, tan color, Royal Mod. 450 or equal.
- 1 each, typewriter, IBM selectric, 10" carriage, carbon ribbon cartridge, Pica Gothic type, red color.
- 1 each, lathe, toolroom, 5' bed, 28" between centers, 13" swing, 1 1/16" max. collet size, flat belt drive, 4-step cone pulleys, 8 spindle speeds.

- 6 each, screwdriver, Philips, #2 point 4" blade, plastic handle, Stanley #P24 or equal.
- 1 each, electric hand drill, 1/4" chuck capacity, heavy duty, speed 1700 RPM, Black & Decker #D465 or equal.

Proper installation of equipment is necessary to assure safe and efficient operation. Some equipment is simple to install and may be set up and put into operation by the teacher or by maintenance personnel. Highly sophisticated and complex units, such as computers, some printing presses, etc., are installed only by expert technical specialists, usually employed by the supplier, with installation included in the quoted price of the equipment. Other power equipment may require the services of electricians, pipefitters, welders, and like craftsmen. Great care should be taken to make sure that all safety devices are in place and operating, since failure to do so constitutes negligence and creates liability for both the administrator and the educational institution.

## PURCHASING SUPPLIES

It is necessary to provide an initial stock of material and supplies for the beginning of many courses. In some instances, considerable savings may be realized if accurate estimates can be made so that the total needed quantity can be purchased at one time. However, if the administrator is unsure of the kinds and amounts of supplies that will be used, or if no significant savings can be effected, it is usually better to start a new program with a minimal supply on hand and to let the teacher order additional supplies as needed.

## HOW TO RECRUIT
## AND SELECT STUDENTS

The one most vital factor in any successful educational program is the students. This is particularly true in occupational training where so many special skills and aptitudes are essential. Therefore, selection of students becomes an important responsibility for the vocational administrator. In the larger schools, which have vocational counselors, this responsibility is usually delegated largely to them, but in the smaller schools this often must be done by the administrator.

Prior to planning the program, potential students should have been identified. Unfortunately, too often this is not done, on the assumption that there will be a sufficient number of interested students with the proper aptitudes and abilities who will want to take the course. If the target population has been identified, the next step is to recruit applicants.

There are several methods of recruitment that have proven effective in selection of students. First, the availability of an opportunity to learn a salable skill must be advertised to prospective applicants. This can be done by any combination of the following means:

Bulletin board announcements
Posters in hallways
Public announcement by public address system
Teacher-led class discussion
Group guidance meetings
Assembly programs
Individual conferences
Publication in the school paper

Second, prepare the selection criteria. Factors to be considered are interest, aptitude, ability, likelihood of employment upon completion of training, etc. Included here is the selection guide developed by the author which has been used for the past six years and has proven very successful in placing qualified students in training courses for which they are fitted and in which they are successful.

## GUIDE FOR STUDENT RECRUITMENT, SELECTION, AND PLACEMENT

The guidance, recruitment, and selection of students for enrollment in occupational education is the joint responsibility of every teacher, counselor, and administrator. However, by the nature of his assignment, the greatest responsibility for these guidance functions rests with the vocational counselor. In order to successfully perform this assignment the vocational counselor must have the assistance of, and work cooperatively with, all other staff members.

Selection and placement of students in occupational education classes is delegated to the vocational counselor, and all students desiring to enroll in any vocational courses are referred to him for guidance in selecting their courses. In selecting and assigning students to occupational courses the following criteria shall be considered:

## A. Interest

Interest is one of the most important factors in any learning. It is important not to confuse interest with curiosity. In assisting the student in selecting his educational courses, the vocational counselor should determine the extent of interest the student has in learning the occupation. It is not safe to assume that the student has adequate knowledge of the kinds of activities involved in any particular occupation. In many schools today there are classes in occupational investigation and exploration. Students who have completed these courses usually have a fairly comprehensive knowledge concerning the occupation upon which to base a choice; however, many students do not take this course. The counselor in his interview with the student should, through questioning, determine the extent of the student's knowledge of the occupation and make sure he understands the manner of training he can expect from the course. Sometimes the student will apply for admission to a vocational class just to be with a special friend, or because he believes it to be a "snap" course which requires little effort to pass. Often a boy will apply for the auto mechanic course with the intention of building himself a "hot rod." When he learns that the course consists in learning to repair cars according to standard specifications and that he will not be allowed to build his hot rod, he is not interested in taking the course.

There are a number of instruments which can determine one's interest. Among the foremost of these are the Kuder Interest Inventory, which is available for several grade levels, and the Ohio Vocational Interest Survey (OVIS).

## B. Aptitude

Aptitudes are also an important factor in occupational education and can greatly affect the success of a student in learning an occupation. Lack of aptitude can be overcome only through intensive effort and practice. Fortunately, there are tests that can identify many of the most important aptitudes. In the absence of other evidence that the student has the necessary aptitudes considered requisites for the occupation of his choice, the counselor can determine his natural aptitudes through the use of these instruments. Some of the most often used of these tests are the Differential Aptitude Test (DAT) and the General Aptitude Test Battery (GATB). There are also other tests designed to determine clerical aptitude, mechanical aptitude, etc. Though a low score on an aptitude test should not be used to exclude a student who has a deep interest in learning a particular occupation, in fairness to the student the counselor should point out to him that he will probably have to study harder and practice more to attain success.

## C. Ability

Ability plays an important part in occupational education, and these abilities vary greatly for different occupations, both in kind and in extent. Fortunately, ability is learned and can be acquired through remedial study in many cases. Usually there are two kinds of ability that it is necessary to consider when selecting occupational training—physical ability and mental ability. Different jobs require different abilities. Most academic abilities can be determined by examination of the student's record of past achievement. Physical ability is often apparent in case of a severe handicap such as lost or crippled limbs, excessive involuntary muscular movement, etc. Physical handicaps are sometimes easier to overcome than mental handicaps. I have successfully trained a welder who lost both arms and a machinist with only one hand, mainly because they had the determination to overcome their handicaps. A student with little mathematical ability has little chance of becoming an electronic technician or first-class machinist unless he corrects that deficiency.

## D. Attitude

Attitude is the most difficult characteristic to determine because it is affected by so many variables. Yet nothing can have greater influence on success or failure in almost every activity, including occupational training. Most evaluation of one's attitude is subjective on the part of the assessor and usually results from observation of behavioral reaction to situational, environmental, and social relationships. There are certain attitudes that are very indicative of success, such as enthusiasm, cooperation, and willingness to follow instructions. An attitude of defiance, disregard of instruction and disregard of other people usually results in failure or at best little achievement. Attitude plays a dominant role in obtaining and retaining employment. The counselor should discuss this with the student during the interview and, if there is evidence of poor attitude, attempt to discover the underlying cause. It may be the result of boredom or disinterest in the school environment and the courses he is taking, so this attitude may change when he is doing something in which he is interested. In case of an attitude that is likely to create a safety hazard or disrupt the class to the detriment of the learning experience of others, the counselor should determine the willingness of the student to accept help in developing a more acceptable attitude. If he is willing to overcome his problem he may be placed in the class on probation.

## E. Behavior

The vocational counselor shall determine by school records and other available sources whether or not the student has a record of disciplinary problems, and if he has, attempt to determine the nature and cause of such problems. The counselor should evaluate the effect the applicant's behavior may have on his training success in the course applied for, and whether it is likely that his acceptance in the course may help correct the problem. A student who has a behavior pattern of such a nature that a safety hazard would be created by his presence will be denied admission until such behavior is corrected. A student with less severe behavior problems may be admitted on probation if the teacher and the counselor concur in the determination that it is in the best interest of the student and not detrimental to other class members.

## F. Attendance

The counselor shall determine the attendance record of the applicant and in the case of excessive absences or tardiness, determine the cause, evaluate the probability that such pattern of attendance may continue and decide if enrollment in occupational training may help to correct absenteeism.

## G. Appearance

The vocational counselor shall evaluate the appearance, grooming, personal habits, and other characteristics of the applicant which could reasonably be expected to impede either his training progress or his employability in the occupation for which training is requested, and determine if applicant is willing to accept guidance in overcoming correctable deficiencies.

## H. Marital Status

Marital status shall not be a determining factor in the selection of students for occupational training.

## I. Need

An applicant's need to contribute to the support of himself and/or his family should be considered in selecting students for cooperative part-time courses in which wage-earning employment is part of the course; however, no student shall be placed in a course for which he is not qualified, solely because of his need for employment.

## J. Teacher Recommendation

In selecting students for occupational courses the counselor should, when feasible, arrange an interview between the student and the teacher of the course for which application is made. The teacher may recommend acceptance or rejection; however, a recommendation to reject must include specific factors upon which the recommendation is based. Such recommendation shall be considered with all other factors in making assignments. A teacher may not arbitrarily refuse a student admission to his course without the concurrence of the vocational counselor.

In this chapter we have discussed the major essential actions necessary to start program operation. Though in some cases other decisions are involved, the basic steps of implementing vocational courses remain the same: provide adequate facilities to house the program, obtain and install the proper equipment, provide material and supplies, place selected, interested, and able students in the classroom with a capable teacher—and you are off to a good start.

# 6

# What to Do When Developing Vocational Curriculum

**CHAPTER 6**  An adequate curriculum is essential to any course of study and vocational education is no exception. Unfortunately, in the past, too many people, including school administrators and vocational teachers, have assumed that occupational training consists solely of practice in performing the skill operations of an occupation, and therefore no special curriculum need be developed or used. Vocational education, to be effective, must not only develop the physical skills to operate equipment and perform various operations with tools; it must also provide the information, knowledge and understanding that can be used in the decision making and problem solving that are a part of every successful career. Since most vocational teachers are recruited from industry, they have rarely had education and training in curriculum development. Therefore, it behooves every vocational administrator to know how to guide and assist the teacher in developing a curriculum for his course. Let's see how this can be done.

## HOW TO USE JOB ANALYSIS AND
## COURSE OUTLINE FOR CURRICULUM

The job analysis and course outline provide a base from which a curriculum may be developed. This is true whether these were developed locally or have been adapted from those produced by other institutions. If a course outline is adapted, be sure to study it carefully and make any revisions necessary to meet local training needs before using it. If an adequate course outline has already been developed, you should check to see if there is also a curriculum guide designed for the proposed course. If there is one available it is usually much easier to revise and adapt it to local use than to prepare a new guide beginning from scratch.

However, for those not fortunate enough to find an existing curriculum guide, I will describe a procedure for developing one that has proven successful for me and for others. The process of developing a curriculum guide is relatively simple if certain basic requirements are observed. The developer must have a thorough knowledge of the subject matter which must be taught and/or the skills needed for proficiency in the occupation. If the administrator does not have such knowledge, a subject-matter specialist must be used. If it is possible to use the person who is to teach the course, it is highly advisable to do so. If this is not possible or feasible, the aid of one or more of the advisory board members should be solicited.

The steps for developing a curriculum guide from a course outline are:

1. For each topic in the course outline, determine all the concepts that must be learned for this competency.
2. List each concept as it is determined on a 3" x 5" card. For each subsequent time a concept is needed make a tally mark on the card.
3. Arrange the concept cards in order of descending frequency.

4. Analyze the concepts for interrelationship and for difficulty to understand.
5. Group all concepts under each topic in ascending order of difficulty and in descending order of frequency.
6. For each concept state the objective, the method of presentation, the teaching aids needed, plan for application, evaluation procedure, and references to text or reference books.

## HOW TO IDENTIFY CONCEPTS

Every skill to be learned and all knowledge of process is based on an understanding of certain concepts. These may be common, widely understood concepts, such as "water runs down hill" or "two is more than one." Though such concepts are known to almost everyone, some may not have an understanding of the application of these facts to the performance of a skill or solving a problem. For example, a drain line must have the outlet lower than the inlet so that water can run down hill. It is important that such application of concepts be included in the instruction.

The identification of all the concepts that must be included in the instruction requires careful analytical study and will probably require more time than all the other steps in this procedure.

Referring to the sample course outline in Chapter Two, let's now identify some concepts and prepare a card or two as described in steps one and two above. Block I, Safety, has as sub-topic A, "Standard Safety Regulations," under which "eye protection" is listed first. A concept card for eye protection will look like this:

I. A. 1. EYE PROTECTION

    Eye is easily injured.
    Goggles protect eyes from foreign
        objects,
    Intense light can burn eyes.

Dark lenses protect eyes from light.
Acids and alkalies burn eyes.
Shields and goggles protect eyes.

You may be able to identify still other concepts that should be taught in this lesson unit. It is almost impossible to include every concept in the initial development. As the teacher uses the curriculum guide in lesson planning, he will find other concepts that need to be taught and should include them at that time.

When the concept cards are completed, review the course outline, carefully considering which of the concepts are required for each topic. Since safety is a part of nearly every manipulative activity you will find safety concepts in almost every lesson unit.

## HOW TO SELECT TEXTBOOKS, REFERENCE BOOKS, AND TEACHING AIDS

The selection of textbooks varies in difficulty depending on the vocational course being planned. For many courses there are several State Education Agency approved texts from which the administrator may choose. In this case it is wise to obtain copies of each of these textbooks and evaluate them carefully. Several factors are important in the choice of any textbook. Each book considered should be judged from a subject matter viewpoint and also from the educational standpoint. It is best, if possible, to have the teacher evaluate the text; however, unless the teacher is experienced in the educational process, another person with teaching expertise should assist in the selection. Some texts, though filled with excellent technological information, may, because of their arrangement or format, be very difficult to teach from.

In evaluating textbooks these are some questions to answer:

1. Is the factual content accurate and adequate?
2. Does the content include all the concepts necessary to meet the objectives of the course?
3. Is the technical information current and up to date?

4. Is the content organized in the best sequence for teaching continuity?
5. Is the vocabularly compatible with the comprehension of students?
6. Are the explanations and examples clearly expressed in simple and easily understood terms?
7. Are illustrations adequate in both quantity and quality?
8. Will supplemental technical information be needed?
9. Is supplemental material available?
10. Is there an adequate bibliography of reference books?
11. Are teaching aids recommended and available?

Often it will be possible to obtain the opinion of a teacher who has used a text that is being considered and knows its merits and shortcomings. This is usually helpful. In some cases when an approved text is not available, the selection is sometimes more difficult. There may be few titles available with the result that choice is limited. For some courses, when first initiated in public schools, no textbook exists.

When there is no text or when those available are inadequate, it is necessary to obtain a comprehensive reference library and from it develop a text for the course. This is usually very difficult if the teacher has had neither training nor experience in curriculum development, and in such cases he should have the guidance of an instructional specialist.

In still other courses a text may be mandatory and required for approval and accreditation by the State Educational Agency, in which case only supplemental instructional material need be selected. Most texts recommend supplemental reference sources that complement the text content.

Selection of teaching aids can be an important factor in the ease and quality of instruction. These can best be chosen by an analysis of the concepts to be taught. The consideration is the method of presentation that most clearly provides an understanding by the student. Some concepts are most effectively learned through visual instruction; some require a model or mock-up to provide manipulatory, visual, auditory and tactile stimulation for maximum understanding. Also remember that effective use of teaching aids in instruction is a technique that must be learned, and that skill is acquired only through practice. If a teacher is brought in from industry without a background of either teaching experience or education, the vocational administrator should see that he has assistance in learning to properly use teaching aids.

## IDENTIFYING EFFECTIVE INSTRUCTION METHODS

Selection of instructional methods is largely an individual choice. Many factors may influence this choice. Some of these factors are:

1. Maturity of the learners.
2. Ability and experience of the teacher.
3. Kind and complexity of the concepts to be learned.
4. Availability of teaching aids.

Probably the least effective of all teaching methods is the one most frequently used—the lecture method alone. Unless the learner is mature and has some basic knowledge of the fundamentals of the subject, and unless the teacher has a thorough understanding of the subject and is able to communicate clearly with the learner, very little satisfactory learning can be expected from lectures only. Some type of supplement to the lecture method is usually needed for maximum learning effectiveness.

In teaching manipulative skills, I have found this a very effective procedure:

1. Demonstrate the skill to show what is to be learned.
2. Have a learner perform the skill, explaining each step, correcting any misunderstanding.
4. After the student has performed the skill correctly, have him teach another learner by the same procedure while the teacher observes to assure accuracy.

Where demonstration is not feasible or proper, visual aids in the form of films, slides, transparencies, or diagrams are usually the best choices.

Many teachers will learn to develop teaching aids designed specifically to meet the needs of the students in the courses they are teaching. Such effort should be recognized and encouraged because this practice not only enhances the learning experience for the student, but also usually increases the understanding of the teacher and his ability to present the subject matter clearly. A fringe benefit from locally developed teaching aids is that most often they are less expensive than similar aids purchased from commercial sources. However, it is wise to determine if a proposed aid is already available—and its comparable cost—before beginning development of expensive aids.

A word of caution is appropriate concerning the purchase of aids. Unless they can be and are used effectively to improve the instruction, a great deal of money can be wasted on unused, dust-collecting gadgets which lie on the shelf and contribute nothing to the learning process. There are many such gadgets commercially produced and promoted today and the unwary are likely to be sold useless aids.

## HOW TO PREPARE A TEACHING GUIDE AND ORIENT TEACHERS IN ITS USE

The vocational administrator in a school system that has a department of curriculum development adequately staffed with professionals who can prepare teaching guides and instruct teachers in the use of them is indeed fortunate. However, he should be knowledgeable about the development and use-training practices so that he can cooperate with the professional staff coordinating the development of curriculum guides in vocational courses.

In schools that do not have a curriculum development department, the vocational administrator's responsibility is more difficult. He must be able to assist and guide each teacher in the development of a guide for the course and in learning to use it effectively.

Let us consider what a teaching guide should be and how it is best used. The author defines a teaching guide as "a detailed plan that charts the learner's progress through a series of sequential learning experiences from his state of knowledge and skill at the beginning of instruction toward the goal of increased knowledge and greater skill." It should be used as a guide *only*. A teaching guide has been referred to by some as a blueprint for teaching a course; however, it differs from a blueprint in that no deviation is allowed from minutely specified details in a blueprint. A curriculum guide could be more realistically compared to a road map with a journey's itinerary plotted, because such a planned route may find many detours necessary to reach its destination. So it is with a teaching guide. Properly used it enables a teacher to continually check his progress, making sure all concepts are learned, yet allowing him the latitude or option of detouring around road blocks as they are encountered in the learning process. It is the opinion of the author, based on experience, that too rigid a guide, which restricts the options of the teacher too greatly, is practically useless because either it will not be used or it will be followed strictly without regard for the effectiveness of instruction on the learning of the student.

Usually the more the teachers have to do with the development of a guide and the more their imput is incorporated into it, the more likely they are to use it effectively. Teachers will also require less training in the use of a guide that they have helped to develop.

This does not mean, however, that the administrator can discharge his responsibility by merely directing the teacher or teachers to prepare a teaching guide and use it. The vocational director has the responsibility of assisting the teachers, who, in many cases—even those who have attained certification through college preparation—have had little if any training in curriculum development.

To the vocational administrator who wants to improve the instructional program through development and use of teaching guides, the author recommends the following procedure, which he has found to be effective:

1. Confer with the teacher or teachers to discuss and plan the development program. It is possible and desirable to include all teachers of courses that do not have an up-to-date guide that is being effectively used. Even though only one or two teachers may be working in the same subject area, the development process is similar in all areas, and most often the exchange of ideas will be beneficial for all involved.
2. Discuss and explain clearly the advantages of developing and using a teaching guide.
3. Determine the experience of each group member in curriculum development.
4. Discuss and plan the mechanics of the development program.
   A. Frequency, time, and place of meetings.
   B. Develop timetable and flow chart for the process.
   C. Plan and design a format for the guide.

   (Most course guides can adequately conform to the same or similar format. A single format usually simplifies the development process and the use-training procedures required.

5. Make assignments or have teachers prepare an outline of their procedural plans. These will include:
   A. Develop lesson plans.
   B. Arrange lessons in sequential order.
   C. Assemble guide (preferably in loose leaf form).
6 Discuss and plan the use, evaluation, and revision of the guides. This step should include the following:
   A. Notation of revisions needed as each lesson is taught.
   B. Periodic evaluation of the effectiveness of instructional use.
   C. Review of proposed revisions using evaluation as guide.

        D. Procedure for revision.

        E. Assembling finished guides.

9. Discuss and plan the training of teachers in the use of the guide and a program of in-service education to improve all teachers in instructional proficiency.

In this chapter we have tried to provide, for those vocational administrators who want to develop an effective vocational curriculum, a step-by-step outline of a procedure that has been proven successful by the author. This is by no means the only way by which a curriculum can be developed. The procedure described here has one great advantage over more conventional methods of developing instructional curriculum in that it enables a teacher and an administrator, working together, to plan and build a sound instructional guide, even when neither one of them has had extensive educational preparation in this area. It also provides the advantages of being specifically designed to meet the needs of the local students.

# 7

## How to Supervise Vocational Instruction

CHAPTER 7 One of the most important responsibilities of the vocational administrator is the supervision of the vocational instructional program. This is true regardless of whether the administrator is a director in a large district with a staff of supervisory personnel under his direction, or is the principal of a small school where he personally supervises the individual teachers. The basic factors involved in the supervisory process remain the same, though application and procedures may vary.

Supervision can only be as effective as the rapport and interrelationship among the personnel permits. In some ways the administrator of a large district who must exercise his supervisory function through intermediate personnel has the more difficult job. Since such an administrator has little direct contact with vocational teachers, he must make sure that the policies he makes and the attitude he has are correctly understood and reflected by those members of his staff who are personally involved with individual teachers. An attitude of mutual respect and confidence is essential to a successful and effective supervisory relationship, and it is incumbent upon the administrator to establish and develop such an environment. There are several very different approaches to supervision, each of which has advantages and disadvantages.

The authoritarian approach is one in which the administrator independently determines what is to be done, gives the order that it be done, and supervises only to see that his orders are followed. The principal advantage to this method is that it saves time in decision making. There are many disadvantages. The teacher may be so restricted in choices of what and how he teaches that he is frequently frustrated and ineffective. Such supervision often arouses resentment with the result that teachers lose their initiative.

The persuasive approach is often used by the supervisor who believes that he knows better than any of the teachers how each program should be conducted. Therefore, he plans the entire instructional procedure without consulting teachers, then meets with them to persuade them that his way is best. Such a supervisor, though he may ask for suggestions, usually has already made firm decisions, and seldom do teachers working with him have any voice in instructional program planning. Unless this method is very adroitly executed the teachers soon recognize that their recommendations are not considered and they develop an attitude of apathy, feeling "Why should I bother to make suggestions if nobody listens. If I can't try new ideas, why think about improving instruction!"

The third approach is the democratic approach in which all planning decisions are made by a majority of the teachers with the supervisor acting as the coordinator. This procedure has the advantage of involving all the teachers and may stimulate interest and initiative, but unless some control is exercised it can result in chaos and lack of coordination.

This administrator has found that the elements of the three approaches can be combined to provide more effective supervision than can be achieved by any one of them used alone. I call this the eclectic approach, where the method is chosen to best accomplish the desired objective. Many procedures and regulations in vocational education are prescribed by federal, state or local agencies and are mandatory. In assuring compliance with these rules the authoritarian approach is the most practical and effective. This can be used in such a manner that arousing of teacher resentment is avoided. The supervisor meets with the teachers, explains the rules and how they are to be complied with. If there is a question of why a particular regulation is required the supervisor should explain—if he knows. If there appears to be no logical rationale for the rule, the supervisor should not try to invent one on the spot but should simply say that he doesn't know but will try to find out, but that until the regulation is changed he is charged with the responsibility of seeing that it is followed. If possible find out why the rule is needed and tell the teachers. Most people are willing to follow instructions if they understand why.

It is in the planning and problem-solving process that the democratic and persuasive approaches are used. The director discusses with all teachers involved the need for planning and/or the problem to be solved and asks for their suggestions and recommendations, which are then considered carefully, many times combining parts of two or more suggestions. Administrative and supervisory decisions should be made after a careful study and consideration of the teachers' suggestions. Decisions reached in this manner are more likely to have the whole-hearted support of the great majority of teachers. The opportunity to express their ideas will encourage teachers to think about means of instructional improvement. Most teachers will feel that even though their recommendation was not followed, it was fairly considered.

Though this plan may not appeal to some administrators I have found it very effective. In order for it to work the teachers must have respect for and confidence in the knowledge of the administrator. If the administrator cannot use this approach comfortably, if he feels insecure when he does not have all the answers, teachers are quick to detect this insecurity and usually respond negatively to it. A director who has this problem should improve his knowledge and gain the confidence and respect of at least the large majority of his teachers if he is to use this method effectively.

## HOW TO ESTABLISH RAPPORT WITH TEACHERS

Since rapport is based upon mutual understanding, confidence, and respect, and since a healthy and effective supervisory relationship can be established only to the extent of the rapport between the supervisor and the supervised, it is very important that the vocational administrator establish a good rapport with his staff and faculty as soon as possible. There is much that the vocational administrator can do to develop such a relationship. He must have a genuine interest in each member of his team. Insincerity is easily detected and can negate all other efforts. You cannot expect to establish a strong rapport overnight. It takes time to know and understand anyone. The more you know about someone's background of culture and experience the sooner and better you will be able to understand his behavior and its motivation.

Homer C. Rose, in his book, *The Development and Supervision of Training Programs,* lists a number of suggestions for the supervisor to follow in developing an atmosphere of approval:

1. Develop an honest personal and friendly interest in the performance, abilities, and goals of those who work with you.
2. Encourage the staff to discuss with you and with each other professional problems and suggestions.
3. Give praise generously when it is due; reward and remember outstanding achievement.
4. Choose the right time and place and have all the facts when a reprimand or other corrective action is necessary. Always be sure the path to better behavior is made perfectly clear.

5. Encourage staff members to prepare for promotional opportunities, and when feasible give suggestions and assistance to each person.
6. Consider and avoid conflict with the personal feelings and beliefs of others.
7. Grant special consideration to individuals in unusual circumstances.
8. Give staff members the benefit of the doubt.
9. Take staff members into your confidence when such action is proper and for the good of the organization.
10. Show sympathy and interest in the personal problems of others even though you would solve their problem in a different way.
11. Deal with difficult personal problems of a staff member in such a way as to assure his personal security. For example: it may be wise to go to him in private rather than send for him.
12. Avoid social activities with special groups who may have selfish interests.
13. Avoid identification with "power" groups until their objectives are clearly understood and known to be consistent with the most desirable long-range objectives of the program.
14. Avoid uncomplimentary remarks about your predecessor and other members of the staff.

## WHAT TO DO WHEN OBSERVING IN THE CLASSROOM

The foundation of effective supervision is based on accurate and up-to-date knowledge of what is happening in the classroom and its effect on the learning experiences of the students. There is no better source of sound knowledge than seeing what is going on as it is happening, at frequent intervals. This means a continuing program of classroom visits by the supervisor to each teacher and his class. Unfortunately, for many vocational administrators who have no supervisory assistants, the multitude of necessary administrative responsibilities and mandatory reports frequently make such a supervisory visitation program almost impossible.

No matter how busy the administrator may be he should visit the classrooms periodically. By careful planning, an extra hour or two per week can be set aside for this purpose. I have found the following guidelines helpful in establishing effective classroom visitation:

1. Visit at regular intervals—weekly, bi-weekly, monthly, etc. Don't wait until a problem exists.
2. Don't visit on a set schedule, i.e., 2nd and 4th Tuesday 10:00 a.m., or the teacher will plan for your visit.
3. Interrupt class as little as possible. Explain beforehand to the instructor that he is to continue with his instructional activities and that you will discuss the visit later. Do not forget to report your observations to him.
4. Observe for these conditions:
   Are planned activities taking place?
   Are the activities pertinent to the course?
   Do students appear interested and attentive?
   Does teacher have control of the class?
   Is there horseplay or misbehavior?
   Are there safety hazards that should be corrected?
   Is there an attitude of mutual respect?
   Is the classroom or lab in an orderly condition?
   (Make mental notes *only* in the classroom. Write record of visitation immediately after visit. Although the teacher is aware that you are making an observation and evaluation of his performance, many become very nervous and defensive if the supervisor writes down his observation notes during the visit. Unless there is a compelling need for immediate correction of a hazardous situation, it is usually much better to make these written notes immediately after the visit.)

5. Look for good instructional procedure. Comment in report.
6. How could instruction be improved?

By visiting regularly and briefly you show to the teacher your interest in what he is doing. By not disturbing his class you do not arouse resentment. By reporting your observations to the teacher you avoid being classed as a "snoopervisor." By commenting on your specific observations and asking questions when you are not sure of conditions that may be suspicious, you will be better informed and invite the cooperation of the teacher. There will be very few visits when you do not observe something upon which you can compliment the teacher. It is much better to be specific in such compliments: "You gave a good demonstration today." Is much better than, "You are doing a good job." It shows that you noticed something in particular. Such commendatory observations should be included in the written report of the visit and a copy given to the teacher.

## EFFECTIVE TECHNIQUES FOR TROUBLE-SHOOTING

When a problem develops in the vocational education program which can not be or is not solved by the campus principal, it is the responsibility of the vocational director to find the cause of the problem and correct the situation as quickly as possible. Borrowing a term from industry, we will call the process of finding what is wrong "trouble-shooting." This is only another name for making a careful critical analysis of all facts, conditions and personality interactions of a given problem situation to determine the most likely cause or causes of the undesirable symptoms. Problems vary greatly in vocational education. There are behavior and discipline problems, instructional or learning problems, facility and equipment problems, public relations problems, and many other kinds. Regardless of the type of problem it is almost always the interaction between people and the environment that is found to be the basic cause.

In trouble-shooting, the systematic procedure of inquiry, analysis, and conclusion will usually give most effective solutions. The vocational administrator should recognize of course that there are problems that may arise so unexpectedly and that are so explosive in nature that action must be taken immediately to contain the situation. In such cases the urgency may not permit a trouble-shooting approach until after the problem has been brought under some control. Most problems are not of this nature, fortunately, and we have time to find the cause before attempting to correct. Let's look at and discuss the specific steps necessary for trouble-shooting any problem:

**Define the Problem**

Until you know exactly what the problem is you can not hope to find the cause or the solution. The more clearly you can describe and define the problem the easier it will be to identify the probable cause. Be specific in stating the symptoms that have been observed. Let us suppose that the problem under consideration is that Mr. Jones is having trouble maintaining control of his third period class. To define the problem simply as a classroom disciplinary problem only classifies rather than defines. A more specific definition might be: "A disruption of the learning process in Mr. Jones' third period class is evident by the behavior of the students, some of whom are inattentive and misbehaving during instruction by talking, throwing paper and other small objects, roaming around the room and engaging in other similar actions, not responding to the teacher's directions."

**Get All the Facts**

The more completely we know all the facts the more readily we can discern the result of interaction among them. Make a check list of questions to be answered. For the problem above the following list could be used:

*Teacher:*
- Does he have a history of having disciplinary problems?

- How much experience in teaching?
- Is he teaching in his subject area?
- Is his attitude enthusiastic? Cooperative?
- Does he like and understand people of the age and maturity level of those in his class?
- Is his ethnic and cultural background similar to that of the students?

*Students:*
- What is their age and maturity level?
- Are they average in educational achievement?
- What is the ethnic composition of the class? The school?
- What is the class size?
- What is the sex balance?
- How many students have a history of disciplinary problems?
- What is the class attendance record?
- Is it comparable to that of the school generally?

*Administration Principal:*
- Is he a strong disciplinarian?
- Does he support teacher discipline?
- Does he support vocational education?
- Is there a history of disciplinary problems in the school under his administration?

*Counselor:*
- Has counselor interviewed students about this problem?
- Does he have close contact with students?
- Is he willing to cooperate in trying to find cause of behavior problem?
- Is he experienced in counseling?

*Facilities:*
- Is space adequate for class size?
- Is physical environment comfortable?
- Is equipment adequate in quantity and quality?
- Are there any unusual distracting factors?

If the supervisor has an effective supervisory program and records, most of these questions can easily be answered. Confer with people involved. Ask their opinion of what causes the problem, and suggestions for solving it. The author has found this particularly helpful when talking with students. If you enlist their aid in determining the cause of unsatisfactory class performance, most of them will cooperate and you will probably be surprised at the logic behind their views.

### Analyze the Data Collected

When studied carefully, the facts that you have gathered, the opinions and suggestions of those conferred with should enable you to identify many if not all of the causative factors. You should remember that all opinions and some subjectively observed "facts" may be biased. By now you probably have enough understanding of the problem to be able to determine the course of action needed for its solution, and you should proceed with the correction.

### HOW TO CRITICIZE WITHOUT HURTING

Constructive criticism is an integral part of a good supervisory program. Criticism is not synonymous with reprimand, though some teachers and supervisors frequently confuse them. *Criticism* is an analysis and evaluation and is a tool for improvement. *Reprimand* is censure and is disciplinary in nature. Criticism tactfully given does not usually arouse resentment; given harshly and abruptly it almost always does. The purpose of criticism is for improvement, and the least hurt or resentment caused the greater the likelihood of success. Criticism should always be frank and honest—but also tactful and kind. Let's see how we can criticize without hurting.

Whenever the supervisor observes or otherwise becomes aware of undesirable practices or performance it is his duty to criticize this practice or performance to the teacher. Notice, I said *"criticize the performance or practice* TO *the teacher,"* not *"criticize the teacher* FOR *the practice or performance."* There is a world of difference in the reaction to the two approaches. Criticize the behavior but do not attack the person.

Here are some guidelines that can make criticism less painful and more effective:

1. Never criticize when either you or the teacher is angry. Even if you are not angry with each other, voices may rise and tempers flare.
2. Plan the criticism carefully. Think through your responses to the various reactions that may occur.
3. Call attention to mistakes indirectly when possible.
4. Use the "sandwich" method. Praise and compliment; criticize, compliment.
5. Use questions instead of contradiction. "I wonder why you did it this way. Would you explain?"
6. Let him save face. Give him an opportunity to express his views.
7. Praise any improvement even if slight.
8. Express your confidence that he can accomplish the needed changes. Give him a reputation to live up to.
9. Assure him of your continued interest and support.
10. End with a complimentary remark.

You will find some instances when this approach does not work. Some people feel so insecure and are so defensive that any criticism, no matter how gently given, arouses fear and resentment. This is unfortunate, but in such cases the supervisor must be firm and friendly, expressing regret for causing the pain but emphasizing the necessity for change and improvement.

## MAKING RECOMMENDATIONS TACTFULLY

The purpose of supervision is to improve effectiveness of instruction. When the supervisor becomes aware of a change that he believes would contribute to such improvement, it is his responsibility to make a recommendation for the change. In order to bring about a change smoothly without disruption or conflicts the supervisor should be cautious and tactful.

Before making recommendations for changes the supervisor should discuss these proposed changes with the teacher. It is important in introducing his idea that he be tactful. Though the fact that a change is desirable does not necessarily mean that what is being done is wrong, many are quick to assume that it does. Nobody likes to be told that he has been wrong, and unless tactfully approached is likely to become defensive and perhaps resentful. Often the need for change only means that there is a better way to do what is being done. Before making any recommendation the supervisor should study his proposal very carefully to make sure that it would in fact be an improvement and that it would not cause other problems. Approach the teacher with the idea that you believe the instruction can be made even better than it is now. Outline your proposed change and present the reasons why you believe it would be an improvement. Ask for his reaction but don't rush him for an answer. If he wants to think it over for a day or two give him the opportunity to consider it as carefully as you have. If he immediately objects to the change ask for his reasons; he may have some valid ones.

If the teacher agrees that the change is desirable, proceed with your recommendation. If you cannot reach agreement, and if the change is not one that is required to meet local school policy or state regulations, ask him to give the idea further thought and propose an alternate recommendation. Unless you have the wholehearted cooperation of the teacher the change is more likely to be unsuccessful.

The next step after agreement with the teacher, or if you decide that it is necessary in spite of the teacher's objection, is to make the recommendation to the principal, using a similar approach.

Your next step depends on your position in the administrative organization. If you are a supervisor under the direction of a director, you make your recommendation to him, along with the information that both the teacher and principal are aware of the recommendation and do or do not agree. If you are the director, follow the same procedure with your immediate supervisor, unless you have the authority to make the decision on implementation. While this procedure may seem needlessly tedious, in some cases it will do much to avoid resentment and opposition.

## WHEN AND HOW TO DEMONSTRATE OTHER METHODS

Research teams are constantly searching for and developing new and different teaching techniques in all educational subject areas. Vocational education is no exception. In the grant of federal funds to the states, a percentage is designated for research and development and may be used only for that purpose. Individual teachers are also continually trying innovations in teaching vocational skills and related technical knowledge. The supervisor has a greater opportunity than the teacher in most cases to learn of these new instructional techniques. The research reports from the various universities and state departments should be regular reading matter for the supervisor, and some of these he may want to share with those teachers who can apply them.

The supervisor should demonstrate teaching methods in the following situations:

1. When the teacher has no teaching experience or training and needs help in learning instructional techniques.
2. When the supervisor has had experience with a particular method of instruction that he believes would be helpful to the teacher.
3. When the supervisor has been introduced to techniques that are unfamiliar to the teacher and that require a demonstration of their use.
4. When an ineffective program is being conducted because of poor teaching methods and the teacher is willing to learn.

The supervisor should not demonstrate when:

1. He is not sure of the method and how to adapt it to the course.
2. The teacher understands the new method and would rather introduce it himself.
3. Having the supervisor demonstrate before the class will make the teacher feel insecure.

When the supervisor demonstrates, the following guidelines will help him do a more successful job:

1. Know the method thoroughly or practice the presentation until it can be smoothly presented.
2. Make sure all teaching aids, demonstration material, etc., are ready and available at the moment needed. If using a projector, have a spare bulb on hand.
3. If the method is radically different from that to which the class is accustomed, explain the procedure and what is expected of them by way of participation.
4. Be prepared to answer any questions from the class or from the teacher.
5. Thank both the class and the teacher for the privilege of making the demonstration.
6. Avoid embarrassing the teacher in any way, either by word or action.

## MAINTAINING RECORD OF SUPERVISION

A record of all supervisory activities should be maintained. Such a record can be a valuable tool in evaluating teacher effectiveness and in planning an improvement program. The supervisor who is faced with a problem teacher will find that a record of his supervisory efforts is an invaluable document if it should become necessary to reprimand or to recommend dismissal of a teacher. It can also supply much data for the solution of classroom problems.

A simple record may be kept on a 3" x 5" card and filed chronologically under each teacher's name. An example of such a card is shown here.

| Teacher_____Date_____ | | | | | |
|---|---|---|---|---|---|
| | Excellent | Good | Adequate | Fair | Poor |
| Instruction | | | | | |
| Student interest | | | | | |
| Class control | | | | | |
| Housekeeping | | | | | |
| Safety | | | | | |
| Relevance | | | | | |
| Teaching aids | | | | | |
| (Comments on other side.) | | | | | |

# 8

# Budgeting and
# Fiscal Management

**CHAPTER 8** Vocational education usually costs more per pupil contact hour than academic education. These expenditures are usually from local, state, and federal funds which require accounting and reporting procedures not common to education in general. In this chapter we will discuss some of the procedures and record keeping that will help the vocational administrator to avoid audit problems and provide the required accountability.

## EFFECTIVE APPROACHES TO VOCATIONAL BUDGETING

There are three common approaches to budgeting:

1. A fixed amount is allocated to a given program and expenditures must be adjusted to that amount. This can severely limit instructional improvement when funding is inadequate to meet the needs of the program.

2. A careful analysis of program needs is classified by priorities as "essential," "needed," or "desirable." An estimate is made of the cost of meeting each need and forms the budget request.

3. Budget is based on that of the previous year, usually with a percentage increase. With this approach it is not unusual to ask for a considerably larger increase than is really needed or expected.

Let's look at some of the advantages and disadvantages of each of these approaches.

## Fixed Amount

The fixed amount method can have an advantage if certain factors are favorable:

1. If there are adequate educational funds available to finance a quality education program.
2. If the allocating authority is favorable toward vocational education and gives it a high priority.
3. If the budget fund allocation formula takes the greater cost of certain vocational programs into consideration.
4. If restrictions on fund distribution are flexible at the discretion of the vocational administrator.

Under these conditions the director has great latitude and flexibility in adjusting expenditures to obtain the maximum benefit. This is an advantage only if the administrator is unbiased and impartial in authorizing expenditures for all classes, basing each decision solely on the best interest of the students. If the above conditions are not met, the budget allocation is most likely to be insufficient to operate a quality vocational education program.

## Analysis and Priority

This method has several advantages and one major disadvantage. Some of the advantages are:

1. The needs analysis and priorities provide a sound basis for educational program planning and operation.
2. Cost versus benefit data can provide for accountability.
3. Budget requests prepared by this method can be readily defended by line item if necessary.

4. Funds can be more equitably distributed among programs.

The greatest disadvantage of this method is that it is relatively time consuming and requires considerable effort by the administrator to prepare the budget. However, this effort should not be considered wasted since the knowledge gained of program needs and priorities will contribute much to better administrative decisions.

**Previous Budget**

Previous budget increase takes the least effort by the administrator, which is the greatest advantage of this method. Other advantages depend on many factors, principally on the adequacy of the previous budget and changes in needs. There are numerous disadvantages such as:

1. Waste is often caused by allocating funds for a need that no longer exists.
2. Without specific data, line item justification of such a budget is very difficult, if not impossible.
3. In periods of inflation even the increased allocation may be inadequate.
4. Such budgeting practice encourages the expenditure of all funds allocated each year regardless of demonstrated needs.

It has been this author's experience that the most satisfactory approach to budget making is study and analysis of needs. This method seems to be the most logical and realistic since it is based on observed and identifiable needs.

## HOW TO STUDY NEEDS AND SET PRIORITIES

The first step in any study is acquiring the data to be considered. Though there are many methods that can be used in making a vocational needs and priorities analysis, we will discuss a procedure that has proven exceptionally successful for a number of years.

1. Prepare a budget needs survey form and distribute to each vocational teacher early in the school year. (A sample of such a form is shown at the end of this chapter.) Ask the teacher to list needs as they are identified during the year. Just prior to budget-making time they are to review and update the needs list, request funds that they believe are needed to meet the needs, and justify the request. Teachers are asked to list their needs in order of priority and indicate those they consider essential. These survey forms are then turned in to the vocational director who studies the recommendations of the teacher, making notes when clarification or additional information is needed.

2. The administrator visits each class, preferably accompanied by the campus principal or his representative, and if possible by at least one advisory committee member. Such inspection visits are important because they provide an opportunity for the administrator and other members of the inspection team to observe firsthand the program needs, and give the director an opportunity to discuss the notes made on the survey instrument. The visits also provide the teacher with an opportunity to clarify and justify his requests and let him know that his recommendations are being considered.

3. With the information thus obtained the administrator is prepared to proceed with the next step in preparing the budget, listing the needs for each program in order of priority. In determining this priority he should consider the recommendation of the teacher and others as well as his own. He must also consider the policy and priorities of the school system, because ultimately these priorities must have approval of the board of trustees or other governing body. The administrator should be able to defend and justify each priority recommended if called on to do so.

## HOW TO PREPARE A REALISTIC BUDGET

With the needs and priorities of each vocational unit identified you are now ready to prepare a budget. One of the most efficient and easiest methods that the writer has used is described here:

1. Prepare a list of the various categories of expenditures for the entire vocational program. These should conform to the expenditure categories used by the accounting department and should be organized in the same sequence as used in the master budget.

2. Using an accountant's analysis pad, list each vocational unit down the left column, and across the top assign a column to each category. Vocational units should be grouped by campus and program alphabetically.

3. For each vocational unit, determine if a need exists for each of the expenditure categories in turn. Write in the amount requested for each category. (How to determine these amounts will be discussed later in this chapter.)

4. Continue until all needs have been included. Total horizontally for each unit total and total vertically for category totals, if desired.

5. Review and check for completeness and accuracy.

6. Type in proper form, as required by your institution, for submission.

7. Submit budget request to the business manager or other proper authority for inclusion in the master budget.

To determine the amount to allocate for each expenditure category the following factors should be considered:

1. The relative importance of this expenditure to the instructional success of this unit.
2. The anticipated cost of supplies, equipment, services, or other items covered by this category.
3. The maximum and minimum amounts that can be effectively used in this unit.
4. The total amount of funds available. While the teacher's estimate of the amount for each category should be considered, it must be accepted with caution.

If a request appears unreasonable—either too high or too low—the director must determine if it is realistic. In allocating for supplies to a unit such as auto mechanics or cosmetology, where the costs are largely recovered by charges to those who use the services, this must be considered if such recovered funds are credited to the account for reuse. Anticipated revenue, if any, should be shown separately for each unit on the original budget draft but may be totaled by program, campus, etc., as preferred in the final draft.

## ADMINISTERING THE BUDGET FOR EFFICIENT USE OF FUNDS

For efficiency in the use of vocational funds, adequate records are essential. It is the responsibility of the vocational administrator to develop a recording and control system for expenditures, especially when federal and state funds are involved.

The format and details of the record-keeping and purchasing control will vary from school to school, depending on local policies and budgeting practices. State education agencies have regulations for fiscal reporting that will largely determine the records which must be kept. Whatever system is used, it should provide:

1. A procedure for teachers to request supplies, material, equipment and other expenditures.
2. A procedure for review and approval or disapproval of each expenditure by the administrator.
3. A procedure for authorizing and executing purchases.
4. A record of all expenditures by category, teacher, program, and campus.
5. A continuous balance by account and sub-account.

A budget management system that has proven very effective for the author operates as follows:

1. Teachers request desired expenditures on a requisition form which is countersigned by the campus principal or vice-principal.
2. The administrator reviews each requisition for appropriateness of the request, asks for explanation of questionable items, and approves or disapproves the request.

3. If the request is approved a purchase order is issued and the expenditure made. If the request is disapproved the requisition is returned to the person making the request, along with the reason for disapproval.

4. For small purchases made locally and for certain routine purchases consisting of many small items, such as food for homemaking classes, a cash system is used. The teacher makes the purchase and is reimbursed from a revolving fund set up for this purpose. Only specified expenditures may be made by the teacher without prior approval of the director. If not abused, this procedure can save much time and expense in expediting small purchases.

## HOW TO KEEP ADEQUATE RECORDS FOR
## FISCAL REPORTS

A simple record system using a single ledger page for each account provides the administrator with instant information on the status and balance of any account, and the total expenditures to date for each category.

A sample ledger page is shown on the following page.

## WHAT TO DO WHEN PREPARING
## REIMBURSEMENT REQUESTS

When state or federal funds are used in vocational education, they are most frequently obtained by contract which agrees to reimburse the local school district for certain specified expenditures. This type of contract usually requires a reimbursement request. Blank forms for reimbursement applications are usually furnished and it is necessary only to complete them.

The information required for reimbursement varies greatly among agencies and among different programs. However, most require a detailed accounting of all expenditures with documented evidence to show that such expenditures were in accord with the terms and specifications of the contract. Documentation is usually in the form of invoices, cancelled

| Date | VENDOR | Requisition Number | Purchase Order Number | General Supplies | | Teaching Aids | | Equipment | |
|---|---|---|---|---|---|---|---|---|---|
| | | | | Expd. | Bal. | Expd. | Bal. | Expd. | Bal. |
| | | | | | | | | | |
| | | | | | | | | | |
| | | | | | | | | | |
| | | | | | | | | | |
| | | | | | | | | | |

| Reference Books | | Furniture | | Contracted Services | | Other Expenditures | | Expenditure Year to Date | |
|---|---|---|---|---|---|---|---|---|---|
| Expd. | Bal. | Expd. | Bal. | Expd. | Bal. | Expd. | Bal. | Date | Bal. |
| | | | | | | | | | |
| | | | | | | | | | |
| | | | | | | | | | |
| | | | | | | | | | |
| | | | | | | | | | |

## SAMPLE LEDGER PAGE

checks, receipts from recipients of funds expended, copies of purchase orders and requisitions. Usually it is only necessary to list the numbers of the invoices, checks, and purchase orders, with the date and name of vendor or payee. In some cases copies of invoices must accompany the reimbursement application.

## HOW TO PREPARE FOR AUDIT

If the record-keeping procedure is designed to include all the information needed for an audit, little preparation is required. A complete audit trail consists of the budget account description or number, the amount of allocation, requisition, purchase order, invoice, signature of person receiving the merchandise or service, cancelled check or receipt showing payment.

These records should be readily available for examination by the auditor. Preparation for audit includes inspection of the documents that are likely to be required to make sure that they are available and complete. In cases where an exception to normal procedure has occurred an explanation may be needed.

## SURVEY OF VOCATIONAL NEEDS, PRIORITIES AND BUDGET REQUEST

For School Year 19--

Teacher_____Campus_____Program_____

In order that we may plan the most effective vocational education program for the next school year and prepare a budget request for funds to operate the program, we must make an assessment of our current and foreseeable needs, set priorities, and estimate costs. To do this most effectively we need your help. We are providing you with this survey instrument well before the time when budgets for next year must be set so that you will have time to consider carefully your needs and make recommendations. Your recommendations will be considered.

### Directions for completing this form

First ask yourself the questions, "What is needed to make the course I teach more effective? Which need is most important to the success of the program?" As you determine a need, list it and classify it as priority #1 (essential), #2 (needed), or #3 (desirable). This list should be attached to the budget request form. The budget form lists several categories of expenditures frequently incurred in vocational education. Not every course will require expenditures in all categories. Mark those categories not needed by your course "NA." An example or description of the items included in each category is given. Please place your request under the proper category. If undecided, state the item so it may be classified. It is important that you justify each request.

GENERAL SUPPLIES: All items of a consumable nature used up in instruction, and small tools costing $10 or less and not expected to last more than two years—such as metal, wood, welding gas, food, teaching supplies, etc.

Amount needed_____Priority_____
Estimate based on_____
Justification_____

TEACHING AIDS: A/V supplies (not equipment)—posters, charts, tapes, models, mockups, etc.

Amount needed_____Priority_____
Estimate based on_____
Justification_____

MAJOR EQUIPMENT: Machine tools, ranges, refrigerators, instruments, etc.

Amount needed_____Priority_____
Estimate based on_____
Justification_____

### BUDGET NEEDS SURVEY FORM

REFERENCE BOOKS: Books used as supplements to instruction, not textbooks in class quantity.

Amount needed:_____Priority_____
Estimate based on_____
Justification_____

FURNITURE: Cabinets, tables, filing cabinets, etc.
List items.

Item _____Cost_____Priority_____

_____      _____      _____
_____      _____      _____

Justification_____

CONTRACTED SERVICE: Towel service, repairs of equipment, etc. List.

Service/repair_____Cost_____Priority_____
                          _____        _____

Estimate based on_____
Justification_____

OTHER EXPENDITURES: All items not included in any other
category. List.

| Expenditure | Cost | Priority |
|---|---|---|
| _____ | _____ | _____ |
| _____ | _____ | _____ |
| _____ | _____ | _____ |
| _____ | _____ | _____ |

If more space is needed use back page.
Justification_____
_____

TOTAL ALL CATEGORIES_____

COMMENTS_____
_____
_____

**BUDGET NEEDS SURVEY FORM ( continued)**

# 9

# How to Evaluate Vocational Education Effectiveness

CHAPTER
9
Periodic evaluation of a vocational education program is essential to continued growth and improvement. Far too often this is one of the most neglected responsibilities of the vocational administrator. Evaluation can have many meanings; however, as used here evaluation means to determine the effectiveness of occupational education. There are several kinds of evaluation, three of which we will discuss here.

## TYPES OF EVALUATION

### Subjective Evaluation

This is the most frequently used and the least valid method of determining occupational training effectiveness. It is only the opinion—or sometimes the consensus—of the teacher, principal, supervisor, or administrator making the evaluation. The human ego characteristic makes it easy to persuade oneself that one's own program is good. For this reason any evaluation report based solely on subjective evaluation is of doubtful value.

## Objective Evaluation

This method attempts to measure effectiveness by comparison to certain standards of quality. Tests may be used for measuring cognitive knowledge acquired from the instruction. Check lists are frequently used to compare the program being evaluated with standards which the evaluator believes to be characteristic of effective education. This is the method most often used by accreditation teams and also for self-evaluation. Objective evaluation is much more valid than subjective evaluation, in most cases.

## Performance Evaluation

This method judges the effectiveness of the training program by the performance of those who have been trained. Vocational education has as its major objective helping the student develop the ability to perform a skill, and therefore is readily evaluated by the performance method. An example of performance evaluation is a follow-up of those who have completed the course to determine if they are working in a job for which they were trained, and if so how well they are functioning in the application of their training skills to the job. (This method will be discussed more fully in another section of this chapter.) A performance evaluation can be readily accomplished if the objectives of the courses are stated in performance terms. These are often called behavioral objectives because they describe specifically what the student will be able to do to demonstrate that he has mastered the skill and is able to apply the knowledge gained to problem solving. Not only is what he is to do explicitly stated, but also the conditions under which he is to do it and the level of performance that will be considered satisfactory evidence of accomplishment. Many persons have difficulty in learning to prepare behavioral objectives until they have had much practice. Most vocational courses lend themselves readily to the use of behavioral objectives because the emphasis is on teaching the student to do something. There are three principal characteristics that may be used to identify behavioral objectives:

1. What is to be performed by the student to demonstrate his skill or knowledge is specifically and precisely stated.
2. The conditions under which he is to perform are explicitly and definitively described.
3. The degree of perfection required to demonstrate adequate mastery of the skill or knowledge is clearly stated.

## HOW TO ORGANIZE AND CONDUCT
## A FOLLOW-UP PROGRAM

There is an old cliche that says "the proof of the pudding is in the eating." This is also true of vocational education—the proof of its value is in the performance of those trained in the program. The only way one can know the performance of these persons is to follow their progress after they leave the training program. This is called "follow-up." There are many kinds of follow-up with varying degrees of effectiveness. Some teachers claim that they follow their students because they occasionally hear from one or more of them and generally know about where they are and what they are doing. Only in a very small community where most young people stay in the community to live and work can this informal approach be even partially successful. Most states require some type of annual report on the previous year's vocational graduates. Many teachers without adequate records guess at the information called for in these reports. The value of this kind of follow-up is very slight. To be effective as an evaluative tool, a follow-up system or program must be able to keep in touch with a large portion of all students who leave the training either after graduation or after some salable skill has been gained. It must be able to obtain response and information concerning their employment and their progress in their jobs. This requires an organized program if it is to be successful.

In this chapter we will discuss two types of evaluation programs. One is especially suited for large and medium school systems with large numbers of students. The other can be more successfully used in a small or medium size school system. The author designed and directed the development and implementation of both programs several years ago and they have been proven more successful than most other plans developed previously. Let's discuss the program for the large school system first, as it was first developed, and the program for smaller or poorer schools was modified from it. The larger program we will call "Computerized Follow-up," since the use of a computer is essential to process the volume of information and statistics which it produces. Let's look, step by step, at how this program was planned:

1. Identify and state the problem: There was no plan by which we could systematically determine what happened to most of our students after they left school, and therefore we had no valid means of determining how much if any benefit the education they had received in our schools had been to them.
2. State the objective: To design and develop a plan to follow up every student leaving school from the eighth grade until five years after he has left the program.
3. Determine what results were desired from this follow-up program.
4. Determine all the information necessary to obtain these results.
5. Develop the instruments and forms for gathering this information.
6. Through contract with a data processing organization, develop a program for computer storage and processing of this data.
7. Plan for the use of the information and statistics obtained for improvement of the education system.

In order that we would have a control group for vocational students and so that we might also improve academic education, it was decided that all students in grades 8 through 12 would be included in the program. The following section gives a detailed description of the methods used in the implementation of this program.

1.    Collect personal data on Miscellaneous A/B IBM Scanner Sheet for active 8-12.

    A. Should be done by students during advisory period—should be used as a learning tool as well as collecting information.

        (1)  Sex
        (2)  Plan
        (3)  Parent or Guardian
        (4)  Present Grade
        (5)  Student ID, Location Only
        (6)  Local Use—Socio Economic
        (7)  Race Code
        (8)  Birthdate
        (9)  Today's Date
        (10)  Street Number
        (11)  Student's Social Security Number
        (12)  Street Name
        (13)  Zip Code
        (14)  Telephone Number
        (15)  Student's Name
        (16)  Parent's Name

2.    Pre-Grid will be printed with personal information and return to student for checking. On the bottom of pre-grid the student will enter his courses for the current year. All 8-12 courses are numbered on Computer Master Schedule.

3.    Exits from student body will be filled in by exiting student when he withdraws as part of the withdrawal procedure. (Student Miscellaneous.)

    A. Student's Name

    B. Location Code

    C. Withdrawal (Mo - Day - Year)

    D. Birthdate

    E. Grade

        (1)    If your district allows students to withdraw without personal appearance of student or

relative, this exit could be done by the registrar or counselor.

F. Reason (registrar will code).

4. Late entries or re-entries—student completes Miscellaneous A/B Scanner Sheet as per number 1 above, as part of entry procedure.

5. Career Development Card.

A. First year of operation:
   (1) Every student 8-12 will complete the appropriate section of the Career Development Card November 1.
   (2) Cards will be turned in to Follow-up Office November 30.
   (3) Information will be key punched into the computer.
   (4) Cards will be returned to student May 1 for up-date.
   (5) Cards returned to Follow-up Office May 20.
   (6) Update will be key punched into computer June 1.

B. Subsequent years: Only 8th grade and students new to the district will start Career Development Card as the card is designed to follow the student through grade 12.

C. Cards will be filed while in Follow-up Office in alphabetical order by Advisories.

6. Graduate Follow-up.

A. Graduate Follow-up will be made by Follow-up Office in September.
   (1) Mailings
   (2) Phone

B. Entry will be made on Postgraduate Card.

C. Information will be key punched into computer from Postgraduate Card.

D. Postgraduate Cards will be attached to Career Development Card and filed alphabetically.

E. A, B and C will be repeated for a period of five years.

7 Exits will be followed by the same procedures as postgraduate.

8.    Computer is programed for the following print-outs:
A. Placement distribution by cluster and D. O. T. code.
B. Enrollment by name and/or numbers in each course, program, school, or district.
C. Distribution of enrollment by sex in all categories.
D. Distribution of enrollment by age in all categories.
E. Distribution of enrollment by ethnic background in all categories.
F. Distribution of enrollment by socio-economic status in all categories.
G. Number making career choice at each grade level 8-12.
H. Number changing career plans at each grade level 8-12
I. Number entering training for career first chosen.
J. Number leaving school before completion of training grades 8-12.
K. Number of dropouts entering full-time employment.
L. Number of students placed in part-time employment.
M.Number of students obtaining part-time employment through other means.
N. Number entering pre-employment training each grade 8-12.
O. Number completing pre-employment training each grade 8-12.
P. Number entering on-the-job training without pre-employment preparation 8-12.
Q. Number entering on-the-job training after pre-employment preparation 8-12.
R. Number entering full-time employment without OJT.
S. Number entering full-time employment without any training.
T. Number completing training and graduating.
U. Number completing training but not graduating.
V. Number graduating without occupational training.
W.Number entering post-secondary training.

X. Number entering degree programs.

Y. Number completing degree programs.

Z. Number completing post-secondary technical training less than Bachelor degree.

AA.  Number entering armed forces.

BB.  Number terminating who are not in labor force.

CC.  Reason not in labor force: health, marital, economic, lack of salable skill, lack of interest, other.

DD.  Number entering armed forces who utilize skills developed through occupational training.

EE.  Number employed in occupational field for which trained.

FF.  Number entering occupation in related field.

GG.  Number entering employment in non-training related occupation.

HH.  Number employed part-time only.

II.   Number unemployed.

JJ.   Number employed satisfactorily prior to completion.

KK.  Average rate of compensation by occupational category at entry, 1 year, 3 years, 5 years.

LL.  Average of advancement by occupational category at 6 months, 1 year, 2 years, 5 years.

MM. Number changing career occupation after completion of training.

NN.  Number returning for additional training after graduation or primary completion.

OO.  Total data on each pupil.

9.  Use of Statistical Data compiled from Follow-up Study.

A. To emphasize the development of salable skills as the primary objective of occupational education.

B. To show local and state boards of education evidence of the scope and effectiveness of a career awareness program.

C. To show members of legislature and of legislative committees the effectiveness of funds appropriated in providing the desired educational outcome.

D. With advisory councils to demonstrate evidence of placement and as a factor in determining need or lack of need for new programs or for need of redirection of existing courses.

E. As a promotional medium to stimulate industry and the business community to increase participation and support of occupational education by providing placement opportunities both for on-the-job training and after completion.

F. To up-grade the image of occupational education at local and/or state level.

G. In-service workshops for local directors and supervisors of vocational education to focus attention on:

    (1) Employment and placement trends.

    (2) Reasons for effective or ineffective placement.

    (3) Identification of courses with marginal value.

    (4) Identification of causes for non-completion of training.

    (5) Identification of programs which are strongly effective in a particular aspect of career development and training so that others may profit from their experiences.

H. S.E.A. consultants in conferring with local districts as a guide to recognition of need for establishment, redirection or elimination of occupational training courses.

I. Planning new schools and in redirection or expansion of existing ones.

J. Guidance of students to indicate relative opportunities in various fields for a particular geographic area, and as an indicator of the effectiveness of the training opportunities available.

K. As an evaluation tool to identify the strengths and weaknesses in local programs.

    (1) By local employment agencies as a source of information concerning available trainee labor force.

*Footnote:* Mrs. Wilma McCrury, Job Placement and Follow-up Coordinator for the Harlandale Public Schools in San Antonio, Texas assisted in the planning and development of this program and is largely responsible for the implementation and the methods used. The author acknowledges and appreciates her assistance in making this program a success.

For smaller districts or those who cannot afford the cost of computerization of follow-up data, the program described above may be modified so that it can be conducted manually. The information collected remains the same. However, instead of being coded for computer input, the data is recorded on cards and filed. The major restriction for this type of follow-up system is the difficulty of retrieving the data and in computing statistically. It is simply not feasible to attempt to manually make as complete a statistical analysis as is possible with computer assistance; however, the most frequently used information can be obtained.

## GATHERING, COMPILING, AND ANALYZING DATA

Gathering of the data has been mentioned in a previous section. The forms are distributed to the advisory teachers who conduct a supervised completion by the students. These are in turn entered into the files and/or the computer by the follow-up coordinator.

Compiling and analyzing of the data, using the computerized program, is very simple. You merely determine the reports that you want and get a print-out with the statistics requested shown in tabulated form. If you are using the manual type program the problem is quite different. The method of compilation that has proven most successful for the author is described below.

Using the cards arranged in alphabetical order, and an analysis pad, write the names of the students in the left-hand column and the description of the information desired across the top of the columns. You may have to piece two or more sheets together to obtain the number of categories you must compile. Each card is systematically recorded on this pad. Added vertically it gives a total of each category. Horizontally this shows a profile of each student.

From this compiled data can be determined all the statistics listed under the computer analysis—however, with much greater effort. The extent to which statistical analysis can be made depends upon the statistical knowledge of the administrator. If the administrator is not knowledgeable of statistical methods perhaps another person on the staff is. Another possibility in this case is that a math teacher employed by the district can be enlisted to make the necessary computations.

# 10

# Effectively Promoting and Updating Vocational Education

# 10

If you want your vocational education program to grow and develop into an effective part of the school and community, you must learn to promote it. It is not difficult to promote vocational education. In fact, since the results of most vocational courses are much more visible and tangible than the achievement in academic courses, it is much easier to promote.

## PROMOTING PRACTICES WITH OTHER TEACHERS

Probably one of the first and most important groups with which the administrator should promote vocational education is other members of the school staff. Unfortunately, there has often been a lack of rapport between vocational teachers and academic teachers in the past, and in some schools it exists today. There are several causes for this feeling of suspicion and distrust. Traditionally, earning a living with one's hands has had some stigma attached to it. Many vocational teachers, especially those who teach trade and industrial courses, have had less formal education than is required for academic teachers. These two influences can lead to a feeling of condescension, jealousy, and inferiority on the part of some members of both groups. No school can develop to its maximum potential effectiveness if there is dissension and lack of respect among the faculty. The vocational administrator can and should take the lead in developing a more harmonious relationship. In this endeavor the following steps are helpful.

1. Make sure that his own attitude toward vocational education is an appreciation of its importance and that neither by his behavior nor his words does he indicate a feeling that the vocational program is less valuable than the academic program.

2. Encourage the vocational teachers to participate in all school activities and professional associations.

3. Encourage academic teachers to visit the vocational classes to learn firsthand about the skills that are being taught.

4. There are many ways in which vocational teachers and academic teachers can cooperate to provide a better learning experience for students. The math teacher and shop teacher can cooperate by assigning the type of problems frequently used in the trade being taught. The English teacher can grade a report prepared for a vocational class assignment and allow credit for it.

5. Encourage a display of items produced by vocational students.

6. See that teachers are familiar with all the courses offered in the school.

## INFORMING PARENTS

Informed parents can be one of the most effective means of promoting vocational education in the schools. Parents who understand the opportunities provided for the students to develop salable skills and who appreciate the importance of preparation for earning a living are usually most helpful in motivating their children to successful achievement in school. The PTA offers an excellent opportunity for informing those parents who participate in this organization. Regrettably, many of the parents who most need to know about vocational education are not active members of this group. Brochures sent home by students help—if they get home and are read by the parents. An open house, held in the evening, is one very effective means of informing parents and other members of the community. Planning an open house will be discussed later in this chapter. Newspaper, radio and television publicity will reach many parents and may stimulate them to seek more information. An enthusiastic student enrolled in a vocational course and making good progress is one of the best and most effective promoters, not only with his parents but also among his associates. Club activities can be used to inform parents, especially if parents are encouraged to become involved in the club activities. Visits to the student's home by the teacher is time consuming and sometimes inconvenient; however, it can be an effective means of informing the parents and establishing a good rapport with them.

## WHAT TO DO WHEN WORKING WITH PEOPLE FROM INDUSTRY AND BUSINESS

Probably the group that should be best informed and that has the most influence on the vocational program are the employers who will hire the students when they complete their training. Too often educators do not keep these important people informed about the skill education offered in the school. Such neglect is a serious mistake since these people can and will contribute much to the development of effective occupational education if properly informed and if they are involved in the planning of the program. Let's list some of the things that the administrator can do to establish a cooperative relationship with the business community:

1. Become better acquainted with the men and women of the business and industrial community.

2. Be an active member of one of the service organizations, such as Lions, Rotary, Optimists, etc. Most members are business people.

3. Make yourself available and lose no opportunity to speak before groups about your vocational education program.

4. Encourage your vocational teachers to join and participate in their occupationally related organizations. Most vocational teachers have had occupational experience before becoming teachers, and many are already members of such organizations. Such membership can be very valuable to the school by helping the teacher keep up to date in his occupation. Members of such organizations are an excellent source of advisory committee members and can also help in providing employment for students after training. Some of these groups also accept student members. Some schools feel that such membership is so valuable that they pay all or part of the membership dues for the teacher.

5. Many companies often replace equipment that has a great deal of service life left. Some will donate this equipment to the school for use in the occupational training program for only the tax credit they can get for a contribution. Encourage this practice because it not only benefits the students who use the equipment, it also develops an interest in and closer cooperation with the school. Always write a letter of appreciation for such contributions.

6. Patronize the business people in your community in the purchasing of material and supplies if you can get approximately equal value.

7. Invite selected persons employed in the occupations for which training is offered to serve on advisory committees.

## HOW TO INFORM STUDENTS

Many methods of informing students have been tried, with varying degrees of success. These range from announcement over the public address system to individual counseling, and include printed information, posters, slide or film shows, guided tours, etc. No single method can insure that every student will be well informed. Far too many students seem to have little interest in choosing which subject they take, provided it is easy to "pass."

One of the most effective means of informing students is through other students who are enrolled in the vocational classes. The effectiveness of this method depends very largely on the teacher. If the teacher is enthusiastic, makes the instruction interesting, has the respect of his students and will stimulate pride in successful achievement, the students in this class will tell other students. With permission of the principal and the cooperation of other teachers, students can be invited to visit the vocational classes during their free period. This should be planned so that only a small group comes at one time. Such visits let the students learn firsthand about the activities of the vocational program.

## YOUTH LEADERSHIP CLUBS

For most vocational programs there are associated clubs designed to promote and develop leadership abilities in the students. Two of the oldest of these are the Future Homemakers of America (FHA) for the home economics program and the Future Farmers of America (FFA) for the vocational agriculture program. Others are Vocational Industrial Clubs of America (VICA) for industrial education, and Distributive Club of America (DECA) for the distributive education students. Most of these clubs have local, state, and national organizations which provide for contests and workshops for leadership training with awards and trophies for outstanding achievement. Teachers are encouraged, in some states mandated, to organize a club as an integral part of the instructional program. The success of such clubs depends largely on the enthusiasm and leadership of the teacher. Properly conducted, such experiences contribute much to the development of proper attitudes and leadership ability among the students.

Leadership clubs can also provide a great deal of promotional publicity for vocational education. Announcements of actvities, public recognition of contest winners and other outstanding achievements by club members help attract favorable attention from the public. Many times the men and women of the business community are willing and eager to contribute time and assistance to the school youth organizations if only invited to do so. Any teacher who has not taken advantage of this opportunity is neglecting an excellent source of assistance and promotion for his program.

Club fund-raising activities can be another source of publicity and promotion. The vocational clubs in one school organized and conducted a vocational "Flea Market" where they displayed and offered for sale many useful items produced in the course of their training. The first of these was planned for a PTA open house meeting. The exhibit was well advertised for several days in advance throughout the community by posters in store windows, notices on public bulletin boards, mimeographed circulars hand illustrated by the commercial art class, announcements at public meetings and over the local radio and television stations. The results were successful beyond all expectations. The greatly increased attendance at the open house pleased the PTA; exhibits were almost sold out and in many cases orders were taken for future delivery of such items as barbecue grills, bird houses, doll clothes, leather work and jewelry made by the industrial arts classes, pies and cakes baked by the homemaking classes, etc. The club had funds to pay their expenses to the contest meetings, and the vocational image was greatly enhanced throughout the community.

## HOW TO PLAN AND CONDUCT A VOCATIONAL OPEN HOUSE

An open house, when carefully planned and conducted, can be an excellent promotional vehicle for the vocational program. It can also be detrimental if carelessly planned and poorly conducted. In order to assure the maximum effectiveness certain organizational procedures should be followed:

1. Arouse the interest and enthusiasm of the students and involve them in the planning and conducting.
2. Make it a cooperative activity with all vocational classes participating.

3. Plan a display of class activities and projects.
4. Have class activities going on during the open house. Action attracts attention.
5. Have students conduct visitors and explain activities. Make sure these guides are well informed and can answer visitors' questions.
6. Make sure that all safety devices are available and in use.
7. Advertise the event well in advance. Encourage students to invite parents, relatives, neighbors, and other students.
8. Provide refreshments, preferably prepared by students.
9. Have a guide sheet describing the activities of each class and its location.

## HOW TO PLAN AN EFFECTIVE EXHIBIT PROGRAM

Exhibits can be an effective promotional tool. Two basic types of exhibit programs are the school display and public displays. For school, exhibits may be planned with a single large display case or area, rotating the exhibit periods among the various classes weekly. In some schools each class has its own display case. In either case the exhibit should be changed frequently if it is to continue to attract attention. Exhibits should represent the work of as many students as possible, not just that of a few of the top students in each class. The progress of skill development can be the theme of an exhibit, with work done by a student at various stages of training. Such a display can be helpful in the recruitment of students. School exhibit programs are usually continuing and may be considered an integral part of the teaching process. They can be used to recognize achievement and develop pride in workmanship.

Public displays are usually organized for short-time exhibition. They may be planned as a part of a "Trade Fair" as a cooperative effort among several schools, or they may be limited to a single school, even in some cases to a single class or department. The planning for each type of exhibit is different.

For a display at a trade fair, space is assigned by the sponsor to each group. The teacher and students should work together in planning, selecting and arranging the display. There should be one or more students at the display at all times that it is open to the public. This is necessary for two purposes: to protect the items displayed from damage and to answer questions visitors may ask. An exhibit with activity attracts much more attention than a still display. For exhibits not a part of another organized activity, additional planning is necessary. Let's discuss some of the steps required:

1. A site must be secured. Depending on the community this may be the mall of a shopping center, a display window provided by a store, or perhaps on a shopping center parking lot. Sometimes the Chamber of Commerce has facilities available or a service club may permit the use of its facility. The more traffic through the exhibit the greater the publicity.
2. Exhibits must be selected. These should represent a variety of products of vocational education. All exhibits should show quality workmanship. A poorly constructed or carelessly prepared display is worse than none.
3. When feasible it may be desirable to plan a demonstration as part of an exhibit, with one or more students showing some of their training activities.
4. Provide descriptive sheets or brochures to pass out to visitors.
5. Advertise the exhibit.
6. Have students available to answer questions and give information.
7. Be sure students are courteous and well mannered.
8. Have exhibit set up by the opening time.
9. Remove exhibits immediately after closing the exhibit.
10. Leave the exhibit site clean and orderly.

## EXAMPLES OF EFFECTIVE PROMOTIONAL PUBLICITY

There are many means of providing promotional publicity. Listed below are some additional examples of methods that have proven effective in some schools.

1. Plan extensive publicity for "Career Day/Night."
2. Publicize American Vocational Week activities through local media.
3. Promote vocational activities with proclamations by the Mayor.
4. Use information on vocational programs as report card stuffers.
5. Arrange for student clubs to assist in local civic campaigns.
6. Publicize student banquets of vocational clubs.
7. Provide a school vocational activity calendar to the news media.
8. Send local vocational news bulletin to parents.
9. Participate in PTA programs to explain the vocational education programs.
10. Utilize bulletin boards at feeder schools to convey information on vocational programs.
11. Prepare news releases for local media.
12. Prepare articles for the student newspaper.
13. Submit follow-up stories to local media after special vocational events.
14. Produce local television program on vocational programs.
15. Use radio "spots" to remind people of the vocational programs available to them.
16. Visit feeder schools to talk to interested students.
17. Arrange or coordinate visits of vocational students to local industries.
18. Produce regularly scheduled radio programs on vocational topics.

## HOW TO KEEP YOUR VOCATIONAL PROGRAM UP TO DATE

In the rapid and continually changing climate of today's industrial and business community it is imperative that vocational educators and administrators keep themselves and their programs up to date. These changes are the result of many factors: economic conditions, technological advances, change in consumer demand, etc. Unless vocational education is constantly updated it soon becomes obsolete and we find ourselves training workers for jobs that no longer exist. Here we will discuss some of the ways by which the vocational administrator can keep himself and his teachers abreast of these changes.

## COMMUNICATING WITH INDUSTRIAL AND BUSINESS PEOPLE

The best source available to the vocational administrator for information on the changes constantly taking place in business and industrial practices is with the people who live and work with the changes every day. The wise administrator, as has been stated previously, will have established a good rapport and friendship with men and women in the business and industrial community. By being active in civic and service organizations the educator can become an active participant in many of the activities with the leaders of the business community. Through such associations he can learn much, and can establish personal relationships that will open the doors to him and to his staff of teachers to visit industry to learn of the changes taking place. These business men are very interested in sharing their knowledge with you when they know that you will use it to improve the quality of training given to their future employees. Most companies are pleased to have an opportunity to help the schools. Many will, if requested, send a technician to explain new processes to the class and advise what changes may be needed to keep the instruction current.

It is not only the administrator who should establish a sound working relationship with the business community. The teachers should also be encouraged to become well acquainted with those employed in the occupations taught by them. As pointed out earlier, one of the ways to do this is to maintain membership and be an active participant in the trade organizations related to their work. Administration should arrange opportunities for teachers to visit industry and business at least once or twice yearly to see for themselves new equipment and techniques. In some areas an exchange of personnel between school and industry has been used. In this plan the teacher will take an employee's place in industry while an industrial employee will substitute in the classroom. Though this method has been limited in use, it is believed that its potential benefits can be great. Care must be taken in selecting the teaching substitute to make sure that he is at least somewhat knowledgeable of the basic elements of instruction and that he is of good moral character. The sales representatives who regularly call on those vocational directors who have the responsibility for purchase of equipment and supplies are always ready to explain new equipment that is available and can tell you where you can see it in use.

## READING OCCUPATIONAL JOURNALS

Occupational journals can be a great help in keeping abreast of technical development in industry. Though few vocational administrators have technological experience in many of the occupations for which they are conducting training, it is important that they have at least an overall understanding of the processes and practices in each occupation. This knowledge can be gained and maintained by regularly reading the trade journals and magazines for each occupation. It is well worth the cost involved to subscribe to one of the leading and authoritative publications in each field. It may seem to be time consuming, but the administrator can learn to scan through each issue to determine which articles are worth his time to read carefully. The journals are then sent on to the teacher of the training course so that he may more thoroughly read and digest the information on new techniques and products. If the administrator will develop the habit of marking those articles that he believes will be particularly important to the teachers, it will encourage them to learn about changes and developments since they know that their leader is interested.

## ATTENDING WORKSHOPS AND EXHIBITS

State Departments of Education often provide regularly scheduled workshops for vocational teachers that are designed to help them keep up with the new developments and techniques in the industrial and business world. Most teachers welcome the opportunity to attend these workshops because of the benefits they get from them. The vocational administrator should encourage every teacher to participate in all workshops conducted by the State Department of Education; in some states he must sign a statement of assurance that he will require all vocational teachers to attend such workshops when vocational programs are reallocated each year. These official in-service teacher training conferences often include field trips to various industries where the teacher can see at first hand new equipment and new processes. People from the various occupations who can describe and demonstrate new processes and techniques are scheduled as speakers.

Besides educational sponsored workshops there are many other conventions, exhibitions, shows, displays, etc., organized and conducted by business and industrial groups, which can be equally educational for the interested teacher. Manufacturers are only too anxious to show new equipment to prospective users. Much descriptive literature is usually available that can be used effectively as instructional material. Contacts at such exhibits can lead to an opportunity for the teacher to obtain short-term employment in the summer which can help him keep up to date.

## VISITING OTHER VOCATIONAL PROGRAMS

Vocational teachers and administrators must keep up not only with the changes and developments in the technical aspects of the various occupations, but also with the constantly changing instructional practice and methodology. Besides reading the professional journals of this educational field, participating in vocational conferences and other activities previously discussed, there is another effective means of learning what is new in vocational education technology, and that is the practice of visiting.

Visit other vocational programs in other districts or even in other states. Especially select those that are considered outstanding. Such visitation, while time consuming and expensive if long distance travel is involved, can be valuable. Since most teachers are of necessity required to meet classes daily, it is often difficult to arrange for them to visit other classes except by careful planning, and then only on a selective basis. The administrator can more readily schedule his time to permit such visits at more frequent intervals.

The vocational director, being in communication with other vocational administrators, is likely to know where the outstanding programs are. He can arrange to visit several of the most successful programs to obtain firsthand knowledge of the instructional program and other influential factors. On the basis of his observation he is able to recommend that his teachers visit certain programs in which he has observed new or different techniques that are effectively producing well-trained, successful graduates.

Try to arrange at least one visit per year to another teacher's class for each vocational teacher. The use of a substitute teacher may well be worth the added expense in the improvement resulting from the shared experience. The author has, on several occasions, substituted for the teacher, in classes for which he was qualified, so that the teacher could visit in another school. This practice also gives the administrator a closer view of the classroom as it is today, helping him keep up to date. For the administrator who has not taught in the classroom for several years, the experience may provide a better understanding of the problems facing his staff of teachers.

In order to keep currently knowledgeable of legislation and other official actions affecting vocational education, the author has for the past decade subscribed to a briefing service which provides a ten-page summary each week of all pending and enacted legislation affecting occupational education as well as new regulations. This service has proven most valuable in planning expansion and changes.

# 11

# Techniques
# and Strategies
# for Continuing Growth

**CHAPTER 11** Every vocational administrator is faced from time to time with unique or unusual situations in which he must devise procedures and techniques to meet his responsibilities. There are many such methods that have been tried with varying degrees of success that are worthy of mention. Other procedures, though rather common, do not fall under the headings previously discussed. In this chapter we shall try to describe some of these procedures and how they may be applied to vocational education administration.

## MISCELLANEOUS METHODS AND PROCEDURES

Let's look at three situations commonly encountered by most vocational administrators at some time and for some programs. These three areas are:

### 1. Safety Control

Safety control of working conditions is especially important in the industrial shop programs. The administrator bears the brunt of responsibility for seeing that safe equipment is provided and maintained at all times, that safety devices are provided and used, and that safe work practices are followed. In case of accident or injury occurring in one of the classes or other instructional activities, the best defense for the administrator and teacher, to avoid liability and legal penalty, is to be able to show that all safety equipment and devices were available and were being used. The method used by the author to meet this need, though not 100 percent successful, has proven very effective for the past decade:

*First,* provide only equipment that meets or exceeds all safety requirements for school use. If present equipment does not meet these standards, add accessories or modify equipment so that it does comply. If this cannot be done, replace the equipment. Provide all protective devices necessary to protect students and teachers from hazards involved in the instructional process.

*Second,* establish written policy that clearly directs teachers and students to follow and enforce all safety rules and regulations at all times *without exception.* Clearly define safety practices to be followed in all foreseeable hazardous situations, and provide guidelines for action in cases that could not be foreseen.

*Third,* establish a safety promotion program, with instruction, regular inspection reporting, and supervision. Adequate safety instructional aids and assistance are readily available, and usually at little or no cost, from industry. Regular inspection is performed by the teacher with student assistance. Devise a check list for periodic (at least monthly) reporting of safety conditions in each class, and provide supervision to see that this procedure is consistently followed. The Office of Safety and Health Administration (OSHA) has established comprehensive safety regulations, and from these guidelines a safety check list was prepared. (See sample presented below.)

*Fourth,* establish a continuous maintenance procedure which insures that any defective safety device is taken out of service until the defect is corrected.

*Fifth,* the vocational supervisor is directed to visit each shop at least monthly to observe safety conditions, to discuss any deficiencies with the teacher and principal and to report to the director in writing such deficiencies and the action taken to correct them.

It is the author's opinion that such a program will not only provide adequate safety control but will, if consistently followed, also assure that affirmative action has been taken to insure student safety. In case of accidents the responsibility for negligence, if any, can be easily established.

## SAFETY CHECK LIST

Fire                                                                YES  NO

1. Are enough fire extinguishers available?
2. Are fire extinguishers checked regularly?
3. Are fire extinguishers fully charged?
4. Are they the right kind?
5. Are they placed appropriately?
6. Are fire escape routes marked?
7. Is an escape plan posted?
8. Are fire signals posted, i.e., bell?
9. Is the fire department phone number posted?
10. Are alarm boxes available?

First Aid

1. Are First Aid kits available?
2. Are they well stocked?
3. Are specifics for immediate dangers included?
4. Are safety procedures taught?
5. Are safety and first aid part of the lessons?
6. Is there a posted procedure in case the teacher is incapacitated?
7. Is eye safety taught and are eye protections used?
8. Is health regulation #5, Eye Protection, available and taught?

## General Safety

Floors                                                                YES  NO

1. Are they oily?                                                    ___  ___
2. Are they smooth?                                                  ___  ___
3. Do floors have safety lines?                                     ___  ___
4. Are the lines used?                                              ___  ___
5. Are floors kept clean?                                           ___  ___
6. Are machines arranged on floor properly?                        ___  ___

Machines

1. Are pulley and gears properly protected with
   guards?                                                          ___  ___
2. Are controls covered safely?                                    ___  ___
3. Are students taught safety with machines?                       ___  ___
4. Are safe areas marked around machines?                          ___  ___
5. Are machines grounded electrically?                             ___  ___
6. Are machines properly installed?                                ___  ___

Electrical Wire, etc.

1. Is all electrical equipment grounded?                           ___  ___
2. Are switches properly marked?                                   ___  ___
3. Are protective fuses of proper amps used?                       ___  ___
4. Is all wire and equipment in good repair?                       ___  ___

General Safety and Sanitation

1. Are toilets and lavatories clean and in good
   working order?                                                  ___  ___
2. Are all areas clean?                                            ___  ___
3. Is exhaust equipment, where needed, working?                    ___  ___
4. Are storage areas clean and neatly arranged?                    ___  ___
5. Are there facilities for obtaining materials
   which are stored high, i.e., ladders, in good
   condition?                                                      ___  ___
6. Are oily rags and other highly combustible
   materials left around the area?                                 ___  ___

## 2. Field Trips, or Visits to Industry

Such trips by vocational students are or should be of concern to administrators of vocational education. When properly used such visits provide an invaluable aid to pre-employment training. There are, however, too many instances in which most of the benefit is lost due to poor planning, lack of preparation, and inadequate coordination of these instructional activities. One of the major obstacles to an extensive field trip program is the problem of providing adequate transportation at reasonable cost. A plan has been devised by the author and his teachers that is in the process of being implemented and that is expected to greatly improve the effectiveness of industrial visitation at a greatly reduced cost. A description of this plan, for those who may wish to adapt any part of it to their program, follows.

A school bus, which had become unreliable for regular service in pupil transportation and uneconomical to repair commercially, was transferred to the vocational department. The auto mechanic class, using the bus as an instructional project, completely reconditioned the mechanical components, using parts purchased at school discount, used components rebuilt by the class, and some parts salvaged from other school buses. With no labor cost we now had a bargain vehicle which could be used for transportation for field trips. It is available to any vocational teacher who meets the following requirements:

A. Qualifies to operate a school bus. In our state, school bus drivers are required to have a valid chauffeur's license, a physical examination and certificate of physical fitness to drive, a good driving record verified by the traffic law enforcement agency of the state, and must be covered by insurance to drive a passenger bus. Upon presentation of other credentials to the transportation department of the school the teacher is placed under the blanket insurance policy carried on all school bus drivers and is approved to operate a school bus.

B. Arranges with industry for visitation by his students, obtains permission of the principal and of the students' parents to leave school for this purpose, plans and conducts pre-visit preparation for the students to brief them on the purpose of the visit and give them instruction for observation, submits a request for approval of the trip and scheduling of transportation to the vocational supervisor. This request describes the proposed visit, its purpose and the plans for conducting it. Upon approval by the supervisor or director, the bus is scheduled for the trip. Upon completion of the visit, the teacher holds a review session to determine what learning was accomplished and to answer students' questions about what they observed. The teacher then makes a report to the supervisor on the effectiveness of the visit. The bus is scheduled on a first-come first-served basis among all qualified and approved vocational teachers, with assignment only through the vocational supervisor or director.

The auto mechanic class will maintain the bus with inspections before and after each use. Each driver reports after each trip the miles driven and any difficulty experienced with the bus operation. Though this plan has had little trial at this time it is believed that it will greatly enhance the use of this instructional tool.

## 3. Coordinating Student Skills for Program Improvement

This is a strategy that can have many benefits to the program and is not too difficult to accomplish if a cooperative attitude is cultivated among the vocational staff. Some of the benefits that can be expected are:

1. More realistic work experience since it is productive and useful.
2. Better recognition of the vocational program.
3. More economical operation in maintenance and repair of equipment.
4. Increased interest and enthusiasm among students and teachers.

Let's look at some examples of this practice:

1. The refrigerator in a home-making laboratory needs repair. Instead of sending out for a repairman, the refrigeration class repairs it. This gives these students exactly the same kind of service experience they will have when employed.

2. The drafting class needed new drafting tables and drafting machines, which cost approximately $80 each. There were insufficient funds budgeted to purchase all twenty tables and also drafting machines. The drafting class prepared working drawings of the tables with complete specifications equal to or better than those they intended to purchase. The welding and machine shops set up a production line and produced the table frames, the cabinet class made the drawing boards, then the painting class primed and painted them. The net cost was approximately $15 each for material. This saving made it possible to purchase all the drafting equipment without overdrawing the budget.

3. The vocational department needed five offices built. Space in a large room was available. The drafting class designed and drew plans for bookshelf modules and door units which could be fastened together to form the walls and partitions. The building trades class set up a production line, fabricated the modules, and installed them. The painting class then painted the offices. Total cost of the five offices was approximately $1,000, saving more than $5,000 over the lowest contractor bid of $6,500.

## NEW AND UNPROVEN TECHNIQUES

The vocational administrator should not be afraid to try new and unproven techniques. All practices were new at one time, and had to be tried, revised and improved over a period of use before becoming accepted. Innovation can be one of the most effective means of improving teaching methods; however, one should be leery of change merely for the sake of change. When new ideas are being tried they should be evaluated periodically over a period of time. Frequently a practice that is radically different will produce immediate improvement in performance but will lose its effectiveness after the novelty wears off.

Before introducing any change it is well to determine just what improvement can be expected to result from it. There are several sources from which new teaching ideas for occupational education can be obtained. Many State Departments of Education and universities are constantly developing and piloting new approaches to vocational education and will provide school personnel with the results of those projects. Professional journals for vocational educators frequently contain reports of a successful pilot program and describe the innovations used in the program.

## HOW TO INNOVATE AND PILOT NEW STRATEGIES

Innovation is called for when customary instruction is inadequate to accomplish the objective or to improve methods that are less than fully satisfactory. One type of vocational education that frequently requires innovation is education for the handicapped. In a class for mentally retarded pupils, most of whom read very little or not at all, reading assignments of related technical information is practically useless. Yet such students can be taught a trade to the point of employability if proper teaching methods within the range of their ability are used.

As an illustration of such a program, let's examine a handicapped occupational training program designed and piloted by the author within the past decade. The rationale prompting the development of this program was based on the belief that students who were mentally retarded should be able to perform useful work other than the very menial types of employment usually available to them. Many of these students, though they have great difficulty in learning abstract concepts of academic subjects or technical knowledge, have excellent coordination and form perception. These students are capable of being trained to perform many of the repetitive operations found in many occupations if proper methods are used.

The first part of the program developed was exploratory classes in order to determine just what kinds of work these students were interested in and could do successfully. A general shop with the instructional activities designed to explore most of the common activities of construction trades was one of the first to evolve. In this class students did painting, carpentry, bricklaying, concrete pouring and finishing, some plumbing and pipefitting, and a little electrical work. Another class was designed to explore service occupations in such areas as food service, clothing care, home decorating, floral arrangement, and similar activities.

The success in these classes indicated that four occupations offered promise of successful training: house painting, bricklaying, food service, and clothing alteration and repair. A survey of employers in these fields discovered job opportunities and promise of on-the-job training employment after preparation was obtained.

Classes in each of these occupations were implemented. Teachers were carefully selected not only for their knowledge of the occupation but also for emotional stability, patience, and a willingness to work with these students who needed special attention. Class enrollment was limited to ten or twelve students, and an aide was employed to assist the teacher in supervising the students' work. Instruction was almost entirely by demonstration and practice. Though the program was normally designed for one year of training prior to employment, this was left flexible enough so that a student might, if able, develop employability in less time and be placed in on-the-job training. Those requiring more time could continue into the second year. Also, if it was found after job placement that a student needed more training in a particular skill, he could be returned to the classroom to obtain it. On-the-job work was supervised by teachers especially trained for this service.

A careful check kept on each student's performance and progress is periodically evaluated by a committee set up for this purpose. This committee assists in the selection of students, the determination of employment readiness, and, when necessary, redirection of those who are unsuccessful. The success experience has been about 60%, which, considering the potential of these students, is very good. Thanks to this program many young people who would have been doomed to a life of unskilled labor or unemployment are now able to hold skilled or semiskilled jobs and be self-supporting.

## PITFALLS TO AVOID

In every occupation there are certain hazards and pitfalls that should be avoided. This is equally true of the vocational administrator's job. Experience is the only way to learn to avoid these pitfalls, but you can sometimes profit from the experience of others. We will list here some of the hazards that should be avoided by the vocational education administrator:

1. *Avoid making hasty decisions.* Although many decisions are necessary, each one should be well thought out. You should have all the facts available before committing yourself.

2. *Avoid conflict with academic teachers and administrators.* True educators all have the common objective of providing the best education possible for today's youth. There are naturally differences of opinion on how best to attain this goal. There often exists a feeling of competition between academic and vocational education that should not and need not hinder the educational process. Vocational and academic education should supplement each other, and with the proper attitudes on both sides they can.

3. *Avoid public controversy.* This is not always possible since some highly controversial problems are too serious to ignore. However, one should weigh carefully the advisability of becoming embroiled in a bitter community fight if it will alienate those whose support you will need to promote the school.

4. *Avoid alienation of employers.* In all relations with those people who will employ the youth you are training you should be very tactful and diplomatic. A good rapport with the industrial and business community is essential to the success of any vocational program.

5. *Avoid partiality among programs.* All resources should be equitably allocated among programs according to their relative need. Equal consideration should be given to each teacher and student. It is easy to tend to favor a highly successful teacher who has a good personality. However, it may well be that the same treatment of a less successful teacher could result in a great improvement. Once a reputation of unfairness is attained it is very difficult to overcome.

6. *Avoid accepting failure as final defeat.* Temporary failure and setbacks should be looked upon as challenges and opportunities. Try a new approach if you believe that the program is worthwhile. Many of the world's most important discoveries and inventions have been accomplished only after many failures.

7. *Avoid promising more than you can deliver.* This can cause loss of confidence in the administrator. Think carefully before committing yourself to a given course of action. As one veteran superintendent used to say, "Keep your corners round, men; they are easier to get out of."

8. *Avoid retaining programs that have outlived their usefulness.* When a program is no longer needed or has become ineffective, it should be redirected—or dropped.

9. *Avoid complacency.* Don't become smug. About the time a person begins to think he knows it all he is sure to make serious mistakes. This attitude can quickly destroy an administrator's effectiveness.

10. *Avoid becoming stale and out of date.* Only constant effort can keep you progressive and growing. Remember that when you quit growing you start decaying!

# 12

# Review Key Factors to Determine Future Objectives

**CHAPTER 12** As we approach the close of any experience it is well to review what has been learned and how we can benefit from the experience. It is the author's sincere hope that this collection of vocational education administration procedures, techniques, and strategies has been and will continue to be helpful to you as you go forward with the development of your own program. We have attempted to present this material in the sequence in which you would normally need to employ the various procedures described in the planning, implementation, and administration of a vocational education program. Let's look at what has been discussed.

## A BRIEF REVIEW

You have learned or perhaps were reminded that the first thing to do is to find out what is needed. You learned to determine the range of employment opportunities and need in your community. You were shown how to develop survey instruments, and how to conduct an opportunities and needs survey of the employment area. You discovered where and how to secure the services of community members to serve as an advisory council to the school and how to organize such a council. You learned of the many ways in which such a council can help—and I hope you learned how to avoid some of the pitfalls and problems that can arise from the use of such a group. You were shown how to determine student interest in a proposed course. How to evaluate the present program as a part of needs assessment was fully described.

After the need for a particular course or courses has been determined you must identify the specific skills that must be taught. This is best accomplished by a job analysis. A step-by-step procedure is described so that you should be able, with available assistance, to complete an analysis of any job, even one that you know little or nothing about.

After the job analysis was described you were shown how to use it to construct a course outline. The course outline is not only the blueprint for teaching the course—it also enables the administrator to determine the facilities and equipment needed to implement the course. The procedure for doing this is described and illustrated.

After determining the needs and computing the cost of a proposed program, it is often necessary for the administrator to obtain funding. In affluent school systems this poses only a small problem. However, many schools depend heavily on funds from other than local sources for part of the financial support of vocational education. The major sources available are the state and federal congressional appropriations. You learned how to locate these sources, and also that industry often has funding available for some areas of occupational education. Other sources and how to find them were discussed. After a source of funding is located it is necessary to persuade this source to allocate support for your program. You learned in detail how to develop, write and submit such a proposal. A sample of a successful proposal is provided as an example, along with an illustration of the procedure to be followed.

One of the most important administrative responsibilities is the staffing of the instructional faculty. Vocational teachers, especially in the industrial occupations, must most often be recruited from industry. You learned some of the strategies that have proven successful in recruitment of these teachers. A procedure for screening and qualifying applicants was discussed in detail. Questions that can be used to help assess an applicant's likelihood of success as a teacher are given.

Newly recruited teachers must often be oriented to the teaching profession. An outline of the points to be covered should help in providing this orientation. In-service training for all teachers is a must if an occupational education program is to be kept up to date. How to develop such a program was described.

The procedure for implementing a vocational program is discussed fully. Planning the facilities and building or remodeling is usually an early step in this implementation process, and you learned that planning guides were available and where they could be obtained. Equipment selection and purchase procedures were described. Several strategies for recruiting students were listed and criteria for student selection were discussed in detail.

A step-by-step procedure for developing a curriculum guide is given in Chapter Six. You were shown how to evaluate technical textbooks and reference material and how to identify effective methods of instruction. A procedure is explained for having a group of teachers prepare study guides under supervision. A guide thus prepared by the teacher is more likely to be used.

Adequate and effective supervision is a part of any successful occupational education program. This is true in both large and small school systems. In a large system the administrator delegates this responsibility to one or more vocational supervisors. In the small district often the administrator performs the supervision. In either case it is important that he have a thorough understanding of the supervisory function and the procedures for implementing it. A mutual respect and confidence between teachers and the administrator is essential to successful supervision. The authoritative, the persuasive, and the democratic approaches were discussed. You learned the advantages that can result from the molding of the best parts of all three approaches, which is sometimes called the "eclectic" approach.

You learned that rapport with your staff requires interest on your part. Praise when due, recognition of good work, only constructive criticism, and a willingness to listen to the teacher's problems and ideas are the pathway to a good relationship.

It is hoped that you learned effective classroom observation techniques and how to develop and use a check list to record observation. Trouble-shooting is a logical and analytical approach to problem solving. An outline of trouble-shooting procedures was given and explained.

Tactful criticism techniques were described and discussed. Guidelines for a diplomatic critical interview were given. A sample of a simple card supervision report is illustrated at the end of this chapter (Chapter 7).

Budgeting and fund management is an important responsibility of the vocational administrator. This becomes doubly true if your program is funded with federal grants which require comprehensive, detailed reports and in-depth auditing. Various approaches to budgeting along with the advantages and disadvantages of each were explained, in considerable detail. A realistic procedure is outlined so that you can develop the method best suited to your program for identifying needs and setting priorities.

Budget preparation techniques are described, including an audit-trail budget management procedure that will satisfy all federal and most state requirements. A sample program ledger page is shown which can be expanded to accommodate almost any program. Reimbursement claim and audit preparation is discussed and explained.

Program evaluation is so important that we have devoted an entire chapter to this subject. With the rapidly growing emphasis on accountability in education, adequate evaluation of effectiveness is essential to continuation of funding. Though other kinds of evaluation were mentioned briefly, performance evaluation is given the greatest space because this educator believes that it is the only really true measure of occupational education effectiveness. This can best be accomplished by following the progress of those who have been trained in the vocational program. A complete follow-up system, which has proven very effective, is fully described and explained. It is flexible enough so that it can be used with computerization of the data or by manual record keeping and analysis.

Promotion of vocational education is a necessary and continuing part of the responsibilities of the vocational administrator. Not only must he promote his program but he must also stimulate his teachers, supervisors, and counselors to do so.

In Chapter Ten we discussed several means of arousing the interest and support of non-vocational school personnel. Parents should be kept informed and should be encouraged to become active in support of the education of their children. Organizing and conducting an open house visitation program was described in detail. You learned the importance of promotion with the business and industrial people of your community and how to secure their support and participation. Many methods of informing students and stimulating their interest were explained. You learned about youth leadership clubs that have become an integral part of occupational education and how they can play a major role in promoting vocational education. Step-by-step procedure for planning and conducting an exhibit program is outlined fully. A list of suggested promotional activities that have been used effectively is included in this section.

Keeping up to date in vocational education is a difficult problem in today's rapidly changing industrial and business world. It was pointed out that it is necessary for the administrator to maintain continuous communication with the people of the working community. The importance of participation in service organizations with them was emphasized. Occupational journals are an important source of information on new materials, products, and processes, and the administrator is advised to read them before passing them on to his teachers. The importance of workshops, conferences, and exhibitions conducted by State Education Departments and often by industry was stressed as a prolific source of new knowledge for those who participate.

You learned that visitation to other schools and observation of other vocational programs can help to keep you up to date.

## SUGGESTIONS FOR CONTINUING IMPROVEMENT

There is an old saying that one cannot stand still; when you stop moving forward, you begin to slip backward. This is true of both administrators and teachers. You must keep on improving or your program will start to deteriorate. Here are some of the things that can help you improve your program.

1. Be constantly alert for evidence of deficiencies in all programs.
2. Take immediate remedial action to correct each deficiency as soon as it is found.
3. Preventive action is better than corrective action. Try to foresee and avoid problems.
4. Keep abreast of new developments in the field of education.
5. Discuss vocational education with other educators.
6. Maintain constant communication with the State Department of Education.
7. Maintain good public relations with the community.
8. Make vocational education courses interesting and attractive to the students.
9. Use your influence to encourage beneficial legislation.
10. Don't become discouraged.

## FORESEEN CHANGES IN VOCATIONAL EDUCATION

There is no institution in our society today that is changing more rapidly than our schools, and vocational education leads in this change. There are trends that indicate the following changes:

1. Vocational education will become a much greater part of the total education system. Many predict that within the next decade less than 20% of available employment will require a college degree, but most jobs will require some technical education.

2. New developments in industrial processes will make it necessary to redirect many of the present programs. Some courses will be discontinued because there will no longer be a need for them. New courses will continue to be developed to meet new needs.

3. General education will become more orientated to the career education concept with vocational education as a major component of the total school system.

4. Industry will become much more active in participation and support of occupational education.

5. Occupational guidance will be greatly improved, starting earlier and more in depth so that each student can match his school program to his interests and abilities.

6. Job placement and follow-up programs will become an integral part of every program of vocational education.

7. Adult occupational education and retraining of workers will be greatly expanded. Most schools' vocational facilities will be used to provide this training in the evenings.

8. Women will become a much larger part of the technical labor force in nearly all occupational fields.

Let us hope that you can use what you have learned here to help you improve, strengthen, expand and administer vocational education in your community to its highest potential benefit to the youth and adults of our society.

# Index

## A

Ability, student, 95-96
Abstract, 62, 64
Administration, 66
Administrator (see Supervision)
Advertisements, personnel, 75
Advisory committee:
    agenda for meeting, 30-31, 32
    first meeting, 30
    function, 28
    meeting place reserved, 30
    members, 28-30
        characteristics, 29
        finding, 29-30
        number varies, 30
        organization, 30
        provide counsel, 28-29
    no administrative authority, 28
    notification of meeting, 31
    organizational chart, 33,34
    responsibility to establish, 29
    services, 28
Affective learning, 77
Agriculture, 73
Aids, 105-106, 107
Analysis and priority, 132-133
Appearance, student, 97
Applications, personnel, 74-75

## B

Apprentice, 46
Aptitude, student, 95
Assembly programs, 93
Attendance, student, 97
Attitude, student, 96
Audibility of expenditures, 67
Audit, 139
Authoritarian approach, supervision, 114

## B

Behavior, student, 96-97
Bids, specifications, 91
Blocks, 48
Briefing service, 172
Budget:
    administering, 136-137
    approaches, 131-133
        analysis and priority, 132-133
        fixed amount, 132
        previous budget, 133
    audit, 139
    budget needs survey form, 140-141
    needs and priorities, 133-134
    preparation, 134-136
    proposal, 63-64
    records, 137
    reimbursement requests, 137, 139

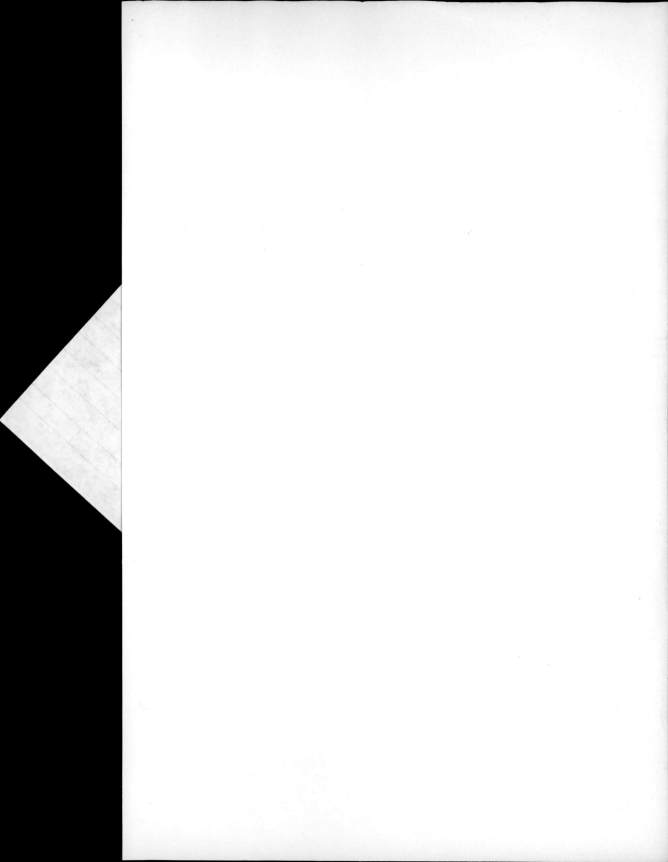

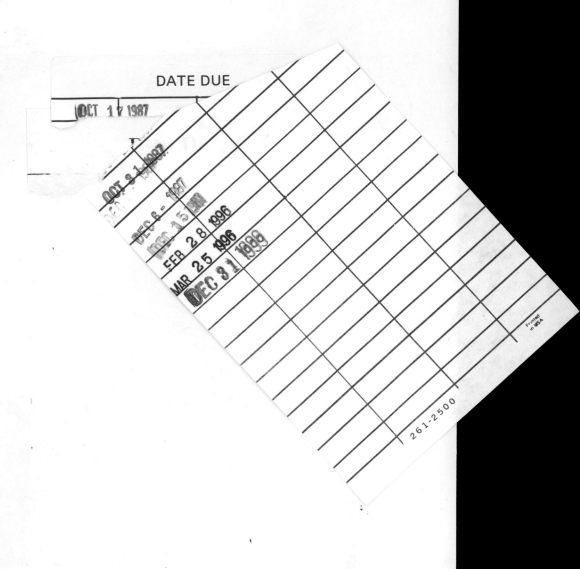